HOUSTON PUBLIC LIBRARY

D0553762

CHILDREN AND MONEY

CHILDREN AND MONEY

$$$$$$$$$$$$$

A GUIDE FOR PARENTS

by

Grace W. Weinstein

SCHOCKEN BOOKS • NEW YORK

First published by SCHOCKEN BOOKS 1976

Published by arrangement with David McKay Co., Inc.

Copyright © 1975 by Grace W. Weinstein

Library of Congress Cataloging in Publication Data

Weinstein, Grace W.
  Children and money.

  Bibliography: p.
  Includes index.
  1. Saving and thrift. 2. Finance, Personal.
  3. Children's allowance. I. Title.
  [HQ784.S4W44   1976]   649'.1   75-36496

Manufactured in the United States of America

Ref
HQ
784
.S4
W44
1976

cop. 1
soc

SOC
R

2,50 pa

To Steve, who makes all things possible.

Contents

Acknowledgments

I would like to thank all the people and organizations who generously shared with me their research and surveys, especially: Aaron Cohen of *Seventeen* magazine; The Rand Youth Poll; Henry Dursin of the Opinion Research Corporation; Katie O'Hara of the American Bankers Association; Mathew Greenwald of the Institute of Life Insurance.

And the psychiatrists and psychologists, sociologists and marketing people, who graciously shared their insight and their experience: Dr. Lisa Tallal, Dr. Lee Salk, Dr. Benjamin Spock, Ellen Manser of the Family Service Association of America, Melvin Helitzer of Helitzer Advertising, Dr. Bernard Yudowitz . . . and all the rest.

To *Parents' Magazine* for supporting my research into youthful shoplifting.

Special thanks to *Money Magazine*, whose assignments for articles about children and money led, in some measure, to this work.

Grateful appreciation is due my husband and children (perhaps especially my children, Larry and Janet) for living with the creation of this book—and for contributing their unique points of view to its contents.

And thanks, too, to all the parents, and children, who spoke to me freely and openly about how they handle money . . . and how they wish they did.

1:

The Dilemma

From infancy through adolescence America's children are responsible for the spending of enormous amounts of money. They do not necessarily spend it all themselves. But the sums spent on bubble gum and baseball cards, piano lessons and summer camp, bicycles and guitars, bowling and a weekly movie—to say nothing of food, clothing, and shelter—add up to more than respectable amounts.

Do children learn anything about the value and function of money because of, or despite, all the money dispensed in their behalf? Do they learn anything about managing it themselves? About budgeting? About setting priorities? How can parents teach the uses of money?—and convey the fundamental message that it is a useful tool—nothing more, nothing less?

In this age of abundance, with its uneasy undertones of inflation and recession, there are no easy answers. But there are a great many questions.

"Alan is becoming very greedy," say the parents of a three-year-old. "He asks for presents as soon as Grandma walks in the door; he knows she always has one. We've asked our parents not to bring new toys on every visit, and they're very hurt. What can we do?"

"What's the point of an allowance?" queries the puzzled father of a nine-year-old. "All he has to do is ask us if he wants something, and we'll buy it for him."

"Carol carries on if she can't have the latest style as soon as her friends do. We're 'ruining her life' if we deny her the current fad. Is her social standing so important that we should let her spend money on things we think wasteful?"

"My sixteen-year-old got himself a job at a snack stand. I thought it was great but now I'm not so sure. Instead of putting any money away toward college, he spends every cent. Should I force him to save?"

And on and on. The questions, as varied as the parents who ask them, are united by a common thread of confusion. "We don't want to spoil the children, yet we want them to have the things that are important. It's very hard to draw a reasonable line. Anyway, if we think it's reasonable, the children don't."

Virtually every family has difficulty "finding a balance between using money to control, to manipulate the children," according to Ellen Manser, Advocacy Team Director of the Family Service Association of America, "and being overpermissive, overindulgent. And everyone thinks, whatever he's doing, it's in the best interests of the child."

The day-in, day-out decisions pile up. There are short-range decisions—"Should I let Tommy have the comic he wants, just to keep him quiet while I finish shopping?"—and long-range decisions—"Shouldn't a nineteen-year-old be expected to contribute toward his college education?" There are decisions we think about, and those we take on the spur of the moment. The effect is cumulative—and it all starts at the beginning, in our fundamental attitudes toward money and in the behavior inspired by the birth of the first child. Is a second-hand crib available? Or isn't it good enough for the family's pride and joy? Does "good enough" mean safety—or appearance? Can a toddler scribble on the back of daddy's discarded architectural specifications or mommy's old legal briefs, or must he have new manila paper for his artistic endeavors? After all, whether it's a crib or drawing paper, we can afford it.

"Average American still best off in the world," cried a newspaper headline in August 1973. Per capita spending in the U. S. in 1971, according to the Organization for Economic Cooperation and Development, totaled $3,230, a figure almost $800 above our nearest rivals to the good things in life, Canadians. We have more telephones, TV sets and automobiles than any other country. While OECD didn't say, many parents would suspect that a large percentage of all three is owned by adolescents. In fact, a 1968 survey by *Seventeen* magazine revealed that 23 percent of the nation's teen-age girls have their own personal television sets.

More significant, perhaps, is the increasing numbers of Americans now counted in the middle class. Fifty percent of our households earn more than $10,000 a year, according to figures released early in 1974. Of course, the cost of living, as we all know so well, is rising at an equivalent rate. But, nonetheless, more and more families have more and more disposable income, rising standards of living to which they react in different ways. "For some," Burkhard Strumpel of the University of Michigan's Institute for Social Research told a recent conference on Family Economic Behavior, "a steady and continuous improvement in real income . . . is a reason to relax and to enjoy the fruits of prosperity. For others, it is a challenge to extend their range of goals even further and to strive toward them."

Either way, more and more money is spent on bringing up children. In 1960 a conservative estimate of the cost of raising one child from birth to eighteen was $20,000. Late in 1971, an equally conservative estimate by the Commission on Population Growth and the American Future put the sum at $34,464. That figure is based solely on essentials; it does not include college, corrective shoes or straight teeth—or telephones, TV sets, and private automobiles. Continually rising costs of living account for part of the increase; part results from an increased acceptance of affluence, a climate in which yesterday's luxuries are today's necessities.

There are patterns to spending, say economists, that are tied in with the life cycle. Newlyweds are a good market as they set to furnishing their first apartment. The birth of the first baby brings another peak. Children are a good market, with increasing cash to spend, as affluence permeates the youngest generation. But the largest sums of all are spent by families with adolescents. These indefatigable consumers—it's little wonder they're the target of endless advertising—spent $24.7 billion *by themselves* in 1973. Indirectly, their impact on the family budget and on total spending is immeasurable.

There's a three-fold onslaught: Teen-agers, even more than younger children, need money to spend on themselves; much of this comes from the family. Young people influence their parents' purchasing decisions in many subtle and not-so-subtle ways; mother's stylish wardrobe and dad's sleek new car may reflect adolescent taste, as the family's breakfast cereal may be chosen by a younger child. And there's a great deal of money spent simply because the family contains children—the sums spent on a station wagon, on a large house with grounds, on a vacation near a lake or near the shore.

Today's children grow up expecting these things, to the dismay of parents uncertain how to stop the spiral but sure, somehow, that it is harmful. Older Americans remember the Depression. Their child-rearing practices are influenced by that memory. "My son will enjoy his childhood; he won't have to work the way I did," a New York businessman insists. Their personal spending is tempered by that memory. "We have determined to be good to ourselves; there were so many years when we did without. School shoes used to cost a dollar and it was always a big deal to get my school shoes each year," a Houston woman recalls. "Now I buy five pairs of shoes at a time. But I feel sorry for the couple who starts out with a houseful of furniture and two cars—you lose something."

Yet today's children and large numbers of their parents—

today's middle generation of young adults in their twenties and thirties—despite the hint of belt-tightening in the uncertain air of 1974, have known nothing but affluence and don't understand the loss of anticipation. Tales of doing without mean nothing to a generation brought up to believe that anything is possible, that all material things come to him who waits—but not very long, because instant gratification, immediate fulfillment, is the watchword of an "enjoy now, pay later" society.

Affluence, while indisputably enjoyable, has a marked impact, for good or bad, on expectations. As young adults take the European vacations for which their parents waited twenty years, so children expect to enjoy the good things in life without delay. Sometimes this even means European vacations. A seventh-grade English class from Stamford, Connecticut, takes a theater trip to England. For $350 apiece, for ten days, these twelve-year-olds spend the ten-day spring vacation, under the sponsorship and chaperonage of their middle-school English Department, in England. "Why not?" says one mother. "Everyone who can afford it has the chance to go."

Twelve-year-olds off to England are still the exception rather than the rule, but rising expectations take their toll in other ways. "Bicycles are a necessity now," says an advertising executive, "not a luxury for which a kid is willing to work. His parents automatically buy him a bike—so his expectations are geared up to the next level, a hi-fi perhaps. As a hi-fi becomes a necessity of life, kids want something else." In at least one New Jersey suburb fourteen-year-olds, owners of bicycles for so many years that they hold no further challenge, roar around and around their homes on motorcycles, wearing ruts in the grass and driving the neighbors berserk. At fourteen, they're too young to ride legally in the street—and their parents see no need to make them wait.

Sometimes, for a brief moment, kids seem to have so much that they don't know what they want—a phenomenon more characteristic of preadolescents than of teen-agers. "Grandma wanted to know if she should send me a check for my birthday," a ten-year-old told her mother. "I said 'no,' for two reasons. Presents are more fun—and I hope she'll think of something interesting because I couldn't think of what I want—and, second, with a check I'll just put it away and not buy anything at all. I'd just save it. And I don't know what to save for."

Despite occasional saving of this sort, a marketing man insists, "Kids know nothing about saving. They don't need to. Tomorrow will be another day of fulfillment. They can spend every cent they've got; there will always be more." Children reared in this atmosphere of abundance—an atmosphere, writes an economist, which hastens social maturity but delays economic maturity—are unable to wait. As they must have bicycles as children, so they must have stereos and cars as adolescents. And so they become the young adults who must start married life with every appliance, every gadget, every convenience, that their parents accumulated through twenty-five years of marriage.

Much of this has more to do with the total social climate than with the goals and values of individual families. The capitalist system, says New York advertising man Melvin Helitzer, encourages instant gratification to stimulate sales. Implicit in our society is the assumption that more is always better. "We seldom stop to ask the rationale of 'more' in terms of other values," writes psychologist Kenneth Keniston in *The Uncommitted.* "Rather we take it for granted that quality is desirable, to the extreme of urging consumer purchases not because they are useful but to increase the gross national product. We are, in consequence, a prodigal, spendthrift, extravagant, and wasteful nation. . . . Even saving and economy are justified primarily by their merit in amassing still more." And, observes Lester Rand of the Rand Youth Poll: "This is a disposable, throw-away economy. It's supposed to be good for the country to buy things, use them and throw them away. Young people can't be different."

No wonder parents sometimes feel that they are swimming against a tide of materialism. "It can't be good for them to have everything," a mother comments in frustration, "but even though I hold allowances down and try to discourage things that are inappropriate—like the cassette recorder my eight-year-old wanted—they seem to have everything. His grandmother bought him the recorder for his birthday." Despite our nagging feeling that children will appreciate things more for which they've had to wait, if not to work (that tape recorder was gathering dust before a month was out), despite our uncertainty about what too much too soon does to their values, we do want the best for our children. And, because we want the best, the bulk of disposable income is spent on those children. "Perhaps," says Melvin Helitzer, who has spent twenty years selling the youth market, "now that the birth rate is going down there will be a reallocation of family resources, and parents will spend some of the money on themselves. But it remains to be seen. They may take the money they now spend on three children and spend it on two."

Perhaps in part because so much is spent on children, so much done for them, some observers feel that young people are growing up in complete ignorance of the value of money and what it takes to earn a living. Caroline Bird, commenting in her new book, *The Case Against College,* about the college graduates of 1973, cites their appalling ignorance of the world of work.

We *can* teach our children the value of a dollar, the relationship between work and money. We need not, in so doing, deprive them. But we must balance the lessons against the child-centeredness prevalent throughout American society.

The lessons we teach, the way we teach them, and, in fact, our attitudes and values are determined, to a surprisingly large extent, by the class to which we belong. Sociologists have analyzed ethnic background, religion, geographical location —and reached the conclusion that social class has more impact than all the other factors combined in determining how people respond to money, how they rear their children, how they live.

The very poor and the very rich, oddly enough, have one thing in common: they spend impulsively, without much thought. The poor do so in part because they must spend what they have to meet the basic needs of life and don't have enough disposable income to make long-range plans and in part because they lack the security of knowing that the money in pocket today will be there tomorrow. The rich spend freely because they have plenty and don't need to worry. It's the middle class, the vast range of Americans located between poverty and excess, who plan, who strive, who defer today's pleasures for tomorrow. And problems frequently occur, says family relations authority Richard H. Klemer, when a middle-class individual marries either up or down. Conditioned to save, to plan ahead, the middle-class person is very disturbed by a spouse who spends impulsively.

Occupation and education, not income, determine class. Working-class people may earn more than professionals: witness the classic case of the truck driver and the professor. But middle-class occupations tend to deal more with people, ideas, and symbols, and to be relatively self-directed, Melvin L. Kohn writes in *Class and Conformity: A Study in Values,* while working-class occupations deal more with things and must conform to authority. The more closely supervised men are in their work, Kohn observes, the more likely they are to value conformity in their children.

The middle class, too, has become increasingly democratized with the affluence of the mid-twentieth century; children are frequently involved in family decision-making and their independent opinions encouraged, at least up to a point. The working classes, valuing conformity, insist that children obey without question or discussion—and perpetuate the feeling that fate is in charge, that people don't have control over their own lives. The middle class, in contrast, feels strongly in control.

Economists have observed, too, that while middle-class people, secure in their position in life, are likely to bargain-hunt, seeking the best buy for their money, they may not be consistent. They are likely to fill an expensive house, that external symbol of status, with appliances bought at discount. The subscribers to *Consumers' Report,* bible of good buys, are said to be consistently middle class. Blue-collar workers, on the other hand, are far more likely to buy top-of-the-line products, seeking, some say, confidence through feeling that they have bought the best.

The outstanding characteristic of the middle class, long documented by sociologists, is social mobility, the urge to get ahead. All the plans, all the striving, all the ambition, are dedicated to this end. Americans are brought up in the devout belief that everyone can grow up to be a corporation president, everyone has the possibility of striking it rich. At the very least, every youngster will do better in life than his parents; starting where they have finished, he will take giant strides into the future.

Because the disparity is so great, the lens through which life is viewed so different, and because more Americans each year are in the middle class (economists say our income profile is now a diamond, with the bulge in the middle representing the middle class, ratther than the bottom-heavy pyramid it used to be), with expectations following suit, the primary focus of this book will be on the problems and concerns of this middle mass of Americans, worried not about feeding their children but about teaching them, in the midst of affluence, to use money well.

These are the people who, seeking the best for their children, move to the suburbs in quest of good schools, open spaces, more living room. The suburbs do provide all these good things. They also provide a series of well-publicized negatives: Because Daddy adds commuting time to his work day, he spends less time with the kids. Because that leaves Mother in charge, she makes many important child-rearing decisions alone. Because the family spends less time together, children rely more on peer groups for approval, a process that fosters conformity. Because the extended family rarely lives in the same suburb, young parents rely more on the neighbors for reinforcement of child-rearing practices, a practice that also fosters conformity. And because suburbs attract similar kinds of people of similar economic standing, competition—that infamous keeping-up-with-the-Joneses—is rampant.

Added to all these negatives—as if they were not enough—is the endless mobility that leads families from suburb to suburb.

The resulting rootlessness results, some sociologists claim, in parents who feel that children need evidence of security, that denying them anything is somehow harmful.

"The Shortchanged Children of Suburbia," a study by the American Jewish Committee's Institute of Human Relations, describes the sameness of suburbs, and the lack of opportunity for children to learn about human diversity in suburban schools—not simply the obvious racial and religious and ethnic diversity but, more important, economic diversity. "The child of suburbia is likely to be a materialist ... he tends to be a striver in school, a conformist ... What is more, he is often conspicuously self-centered."

Yet a study done in the suburbs of Chicago refutes these absolutes. Sociologist Helena Znaniecki Lopata reported that superficial similarities in life-style conceal significant occupational, religious and economic divergencies. Suburban display of outward conformity, she concludes, may be no greater and no more significant than the conformity of urbanites.

For most residents, urban neighborhoods are no more diverse than suburban communities. And, in fact, today's sheltered, frequently private school educated, urban child of the upper middle class sees less diversity, has less chance to witness different life-styles, than the relatively free-wheeling youngsters of suburbia. Neither are all suburbs identical; many contain heterogeneous groupings of people representing different economic levels. "My kids picked some of the richest kids in town for their friends," says one mother in a suburb of New York, "and we can't compete with the things those children have and the places they go. But, at the same time, mine see that some of our neighbors have much less than we do."

It is possible to pick a community, urban or suburban, where seventh graders aren't expected to make trips to England, where every sixteen-year-old doesn't automatically get a car, and where there is, in fact, diversity. This is seldom one of the things parents consider when they are deciding where to move; perhaps it should be. But even those who have established roots in a community that, they subsequently realize, overemphasizes material values can, if with difficulty, stand firm.

The difficulty arises because, no matter how firm a given set of parents may be on money matters, children don't grow up in a family vacuum. Peer groups, neighborhoods, and society at large battle with parents for influence. From the toy that is touted on television to the riding lessons that "all the kids" are taking, parents are under pressure. What makes it more difficult is that sometimes it is important for children to do what the other kids are doing, to wear the same kind of jeans, to go bowling or biking or whatever, to participate in the social life of the neighborhood. Parents have to tread a delicate line between encouraging keeping-up-with-the-Joneses'-kids and ignoring, or trying to ignore, social standards of the community.

Wherever we live, whether we are "richer" or "poorer" within the spectrum of the middle class, in the interest of doing the best for our children, in furthering their chances for success in life, we sometimes inadvertently create conflicts, for ourselves and for them. None of us means to foster conformity, materialism, or competitiveness—yet we want our children to get along with the group, have the things we did without, and win top honors in every field. There's nothing wrong with these goals—no parent wants less than the best for his child—but we should be aware just what our goals are and how they are achieved.

The conflict is basic. Sociologist James H. S. Bossard points to a fundamental ambivalence: How much should we do for our children in our parental responsibility to give them every opportunity for success, and how much should they be permitted, or compelled, to do for themselves, so that they will become adults capable of assuming responsibility?

Out of this basic conflict stem all the secondary confusions that plague us: How much money should we give our children—and does it matter what the kid down the block gets in allowance? How much should we spend on clothing—and does it matter that Janie has two pairs of shoes while her friend Joan has four? How soon can they be expected to earn some money for themselves—and when they do should we expect them to save part of their earnings, or don't we have any say in the matter? Can we take a trip, just us, without feeling guilty because we've denied them tennis lessons?

The questions are sufficiently complex by themselves. Complicating the answers are the ingrained attitudes toward money which each adult brings to marriage and to parenthood. In part inborn, in part environmentally conditioned, these attitudes come across loud and clear to the children. When parents differ in their fundamental outlook toward money, there can be conflict. "My mother wanted me to have nice clothes. I don't think my father wanted me *not* to have; he just never wanted to spend the money."

People react differently to the same kind of environmental stimulus. "I'm very cautious with money because I can't get over my childhood training," says one woman. "I really could spend more freely now but my father trained me almost too well; I can't enjoy buying things for myself." In contrast, another woman, with a similar background, has reacted in reverse. "I vowed never to pinch pennies the way my father did, when it wasn't necessary," she says. "So I treat myself very well."

As it happens, the first woman was a first-born child, the second was not. People's responses to money are affected not only by parental attitudes but by birth order and inborn temperament. Underlying community pressures, the economic and occupational status of the family, parental attitudes toward money and possessions, lies the child as an individual and his position in the family. Freud recognized the importance of birth order; recent researchers have confirmed that first-borns tend to be higher achievers than subsequent children. Early born children are reared more anxiously, say sociologists, and their parents have higher expectations; as a result these children are more highly motivated to succeed, to command parental approval, than later born, more indulgently reared children.

In large families there is often clear-cut role assignment: one child will be the responsible type, one more noticeably sociable, one studious, and so on, as if they unconsciously carve out individual territories. Many parents see the same kind of instinctive avoidance of competition in a two-child family. "Jeff is outgoing, sociable, and lively. Alan is far more conservative, far more involved in his school work. Thank goodness they're so different," their mother says. "Because they're so close in age, only twenty-one months apart, competition could be intolerable."

The way people feel about money, the way they spend it freely or squirrel it away, is closely related to the way they feel, inside, about themselves and the world. Secure individuals, whether first-born or not, can turn loose easily and spend; they have, says New York psychiatrist Lisa Tallal, enough basic trust in the family and the world to feel free about spending, to feel that they have support. Squirrelers, on the other hand, adults or children, are less secure and feel that they must rely on themselves. There's no hard-and-fast rule about family placement, though; other factors, such as closeness in age, also play a role. A first-born son, for example, normally self-confident and secure in his parent's love, might feel displaced by a second son born when he himself is still a baby.

Being a second- or third-born has other ramifications, such as always inheriting second-hand possessions. "I always wanted a new doll," a college student told me. "But my sister had so many to pass on to me that my parents never saw any point in buying a new one. Even for Christmas, when what I wanted most was a doll, they would get me something else. I won't do that to my children."

She probably won't. She'll do something else that her children will find intolerable. But even if she does everything right, or as right as possible, she is likely to find that her separate children react to money in different ways. "I always treated my children the same way, taught the same lessons about money," a woman bank officer asserts. "Yet my daughter is careful, knows the value of a dollar. My son spends money like water." And a mother of two boys notes: "One spends money like a drunken sailor; he goes through his eight dollars of paper route earnings in two days. The other one doesn't spend at all."

"There are tremendous inborn differences," says Louise Bates Ames of The Gesell Institute. "Some children toss money around, are extra generous. Others are cautious, won't lend a cent—but may be the only ones with cash on hand when you need it." Or, as Dr. Benjamin Spock insists: "Parents don't have complete control over how their children turn out. You can get a hoarder and a spendthrift in the same family with the same system."

Personalities tend to be all of a piece. "David is adventurous in eating, and he's a born spender," says his mother, "while Andrea, three years younger, is a timid eater and won't spend a dime."

And the personality patterns which will be expressed in eating habits or in responses to money can be predicted in newborns, according to research by the National Institute of Mental Health. "Infants who took their food fast and vigorously and protested loudly when their bottles were removed were independent and capable youngsters [in] nursery school two and a half years later. Those infants who were lethargic and made little or no complaint when their feeding was stopped were dependent and less competent at two and a half." In another long-term study, doctors found that newborns who startle easily become children who fight going to school or to camp, individuals who from infancy onward are supersensitive to environmental change.

These inborn responses, combined with environmental conditioning and specific parental teaching, create the total individual. The infinite possible variations explain why it sometimes happens that two people who espouse the identical philosophy act upon it in opposite ways. One thrifty soul always buys the best because it will wear longer; another will buy the cheaper item because its replacement cost is lower. Both are convinced they are taking the financially conservative route. Both may do very well—unless they happen to marry each other.

This is why parents who are in basic agreement sometimes, as products of their own childhood conditioning, respond very differently to spending and saving, responses that have an impact on the children and on the family as a whole. "I come from a very conservative home," reports one mother. "My husband's family spends money freely. I'm glad that he does, really, and glad that I don't have to account for every penny, but every once in a while I start to worry, to think we're spending too freely. When I get upset and start questioning expenditures, I know the children are listening. While I don't want them to think I'm stingy, I don't want them to spend foolishly either."

Children are always listening, whether to rational disagreement or outright argument. Furthermore, they quickly learn, when parents are at financial odds, how to play one against the other. "My husband will buy treats for the children," the same woman goes on, "things that I think are needless extravagances. We had quite a discussion the time he took our eight-year-old daughter to a piano lesson, detoured on the way home and arrived with a party dress she had picked out. I know it was wrong to let Laurie hear our disagreement, especially my negative reaction to her father buying her a treat, but I couldn't help it."

Most couples reach some kind of balance, even if they don't always agree. But not all. Martha, now herself a mother of teen-agers, vividly recalls a particular party dress, bought while she was in college. "It cost forty-five dollars. I don't know now whether that was a lot or a little for that particular dress at that particular time. I do know we could afford it. But I'll always remember my mother's whispered, 'We won't tell Daddy what this cost.' "

Most couples don't stay married if they have really serious disagreements about money. But minor differences have an affect too—on the marriage relationship and on the children. Are financial decisions made jointly or does one parent dominate the other? Who gives the children their pocket money? Or do the parents disagree on whether youngsters should have allowances at all? Is one parent indulgent and the other not? Do they settle their differences in private, or air them in front of the children? Where there is frequent conflict, says a family therapist, children can wind up either with a complete disregard for money or terrified to spend, forever petrified of going broke. Where there is good-humored disagreement—or not so good-humored, but infrequent—the children may benefit, seeing that there are different, equally valid ways of coping—and that their parents are human too.

Children pick up clues from parents about money as they pick up subtle prejudices of any kind, Dr. Tallal points out, without words. They absorb the attitudes implicit in the family's style of living as they absorb sustenance.

Sometimes whether mother has a mink coat is not so important as whether she thinks she ought to have one, and why. "My mother noted many times, too many, that she was the only one among her friends who didn't have a fur coat," a writer recalls, pointing up that her parents disdained money in some ways but were very sensitive to it in others. Whether or not the children go to summer camp is less important than the grounds on which the decision is made—and the way the particular camp is selected. "I wanted to go to Girl Scout Camp with my friend," a young woman says. "They went on overnight canoe trips and it sounded great. But my parents thought it was 'important' that I go to a 'better' camp. I had a good time, almost despite myself, but I never got over my resentment."

Where attitudes are concerned, it's not so simple a matter as conspicuous consumption versus understatement. "We never thought about money," says one woman, a lawyer. "It was just there, if we wanted to go on vacation, or needed a car. We didn't live lavishly, but there always seemed to be money to do what my parents thought needed doing." "My parents were preoccupied with savings," recalls another. "They were always thinking about tomorrow, with the result that today was never any fun." Or, as an accountant, with an accountant's money-consciousness, puts it: "A lot of people make the mistake of accruing wealth and depriving the family during the years when they could be doing things together. They work like mad, pay off the mortgage, build up investments, but feel they can't travel. When they finally have what they think is enough money, the kids are gone. They won't spend money as an investment in the kids or in a style of living."

Children learn far more from what their parents do than from what they say, according to psychiatrists. If Dad says, "You don't need a motorcycle just because John has one," and then decides it's time to trade in the car because it's the oldest one on the block, the message is crystal clear. Kids see what our values are. They see our priorities.

At the same time, we needn't always worry about what the children think. There is nothing wrong with deciding that a vacation trip for the parents is more important than tennis lessons for the kids; it's okay to buy new carpeting, if that's what you want, instead of sending the kids to camp. Parents should never feel guilty about doing for themselves as well as for their children.

We are all somewhat irrational when it comes to money. We carefully balance the food budget—and impulsively buy an extra pair of shoes. We can't resist a new record album or a new pipe for the briar collection. Some of us never manage to budget at all, and somehow we survive.

Whatever our particular illogic, and despite the pressures of an affluent society, it is nonetheless possible to raise children with a rational attitude toward money. But there are psychological underpinnings to the structure of allowances, earnings, spending, and saving. Let's look, first, at where it all begins.

2:

In the Beginning

Early experiences, say behavioral scientists, have lifelong impact. The experiences that make up an individual's responses to money, his patterns of spending and saving, are composed of many things, some seemingly unrelated and many unremembered. Long before parents "teach" their children about money management, long before parents even realize how much children already understand, on an emotional if not a rational level, the foundation is laid, a foundation so firmly established that it may be even harder to budge than one built of brick or stone.

When *do* children learn the meaning of money? When—and how—is it sorted out from all the other objects and things that surround our children from infancy? The process is gradual, but before most children enter first grade they have a firm understanding that money is significant. Without understanding how or why, they know, with unswervable conviction, that money plays a major role in their personal lives.

"Jamie's ship models are going to drive me crazy. They're

absolutely undustable, with all that delicate rigging. And he won't part with a single one."

Models, stamps, bottle caps, dolls, baseball cards—children's collections are endless. Virtually every child goes through at least one such stage; some collect many things in rapid succession, unable to fix on one they really enjoy but equally unwilling to discard unsuccessful ventures.

Collecting objects is a form of power for the young child, a way in which he can organize and control at least one small part of his world. It starts early. Jamie is nine, but at two, his mother recalls, he was lining up neat rows of pebbles in the playground. At two and a half, he was preoccupied with pennies, clutching fistfuls when he could find them and carrying them around with him through the day. "At first, when he picked up pennies from the dresser, it was cute. Then, when my husband's carfare started disappearing, we had to stop him. Jamie couldn't understand why he couldn't keep the coins."

No small child can understand why he is allowed to collect buttons or pebbles but not coins. Since coins have no apparent worth for a toddler, he cannot possibly understand why they are different from other collectibles. But, because they are different to his parents, they immediately take on meaning for him.

This kind of experience may provoke the first conscious awareness of money, of the distinct value of coins. But other, earlier and more intangible, impressions may have even more long-range effect. Feeding patterns, for example. One research study actually demonstrated that an aggressive grabbing for breast or bottle, followed by rapid feeding, is rewarded by the unconscious attitudes of middle-class mothers, mothers themselves brought up in a culture that values competitiveness. "Look at that tiger," says the proud parent. "Nothing stands in his way." Surely no mother intentionally fosters a desire for worldly success, for capitalistic greed, in her nursing infant; yet, according to the researchers, the very manner in which she holds her child can inculcate a relaxed, take-life-as-it-comes attitude or a tense, hurry-up-and-get-it-while-you-can feeling, as the child conforms to his mother's unspoken expectations to win her approval. "The child learns an attitude toward the world," says Margaret Mead, "and that anger and self-assertion will be rewarded." Perhaps it's inevitable that such basic personality patterns are later reflected in the child's responses to money.

And then there's toilet training. We may be more casual about this developmental crisis than our mothers were, but it's still the subject of many a park-bench conversation. Despite the certain knowledge that no diaper-wearing three-year-old will still be wearing diapers on his wedding day, mothers still vie for early "success," as if training pants are an evidence of award-winning motherhood. Early toilet training under pressure, actually, is merely tangible evidence of the adult's ability to master the child.

If more young mothers realized the strong connection traditional Freudians draw between toilet training and later reactions to money, there might be even more park-bench discussion. Freud's message, reduced to its simplest form, is that childhood experiences have profound influence on adult life. One of childhood's most significant experiences, in the classical psychoanalytic view, is bowel training, crucial because the child is becoming aware of his own body, crucial because he is beginning to be able to control his own bodily functions, crucial because his mother, center of his existence, is asking him to give up something he has produced. Indeed the child's excreta, say psychiatrists, constitute his first medium of exchange, the first thing he can hold on to or freely give.

You must have heard a frustrated mother cry: "That child knows I want him to do his thing in the toilet. Yet he'll sit there for a half hour—and the minute I take him off, he deposits the load in his diaper. I swear it's deliberate." It probably is, although the child couldn't put it in so many words. But think about it. Just how many ways are there for a small child to show his mother that he is an independent person? That he's not subject to her total control? That he can produce something she wants very badly?

Many mothers, often women who are themselves compulsively neat (because of the way they were trained?), are determined to train their children early, to be rid of the whole hassle as soon as possible. "I have it down to a science," said the mother of Lisa, age twenty months. "She has to sit on the potty seat after every meal, for as long as it takes. I'm going to have her trained before she's two."

Other mothers, more in tune with today's philosophy of child rearing, are equally determined to be relaxed about the whole matter, to let the child train himself when he is ready. Of course, being determined to be relaxed can be self-defeating. Unless a mother truly isn't bothered by her offspring's failure to become civilized in this fundamental way, he'll know it. And it doesn't take words. A toddler doesn't have to hear a lecture to know, by his mother's face, just when he is pleasing or displeasing her. "Adam is two and a half," says his mother, "and totally uninterested in using the bathroom. I try to tell him calmly that when he's a big boy, he'll use the toilet and not his diapers, but it's not always easy to be calm. It doesn't help that he's big for his age. If I have to change his diapers in the park or at the beach, I can just feel the disapproval of others—and I know he senses my disapproval and, basically, my distaste."

Is it any wonder that all sorts of emotions get mixed in with the seemingly simple matter of learning to use the bathroom? A child must learn to hold on to, then to give up, the product of his body, in a specified place, to earn his mother's approval. If she takes the whole matter very seriously, if she is, in fact, compulsive about it (or about any other fundamental aspect of his life), is it any wonder that he, in turn, becomes compulsive? There we have Freud's theory that compulsive, obsessive, parsimonious, obstinate personality types are formed during toilet training. And, as pediatric psychologist Lee Salk has pointed out, people with this strong tendency to hold on to things eventually have to give them up—and when they do, watch out, because it will be explosive. A pattern of parsimony will be broken by fits of extravagance.

Before you say, "Aha, no wonder John is so awful about

money," before you panic over your two-year old's obstinacy, let's weigh all the available evidence. Few child-development experts care to be dogmatic along Freudian lines today. Even Dr. Spock, guru to a whole generation of parents, has modified his once-traditional Freudian view. "While an excessively stingy individual probably had a mother who went after his bowels too aggressively," he says, "I wouldn't want parents to take this possibility so seriously that they are afraid to train at all. Today's college-educated parents are too cautious anyway. I wouldn't want to scare them off altogether."

The whole concept of linking attitudes toward money with toilet training seems faintly amusing to the modern parent. And that may be as it should be, since, as Dr. Spock notes, taking it too seriously may lead to other problems. But, without turning parents into amateur psychologists, it's good to know the basic Freudian theory before turning to more practical aspects of teaching money management.

Both psychiatrists and linguists have pointed to all the slang terms for money that stem from excreta: filthy lucre, craps, the gambler's "pot." Again, the infant's feces may be what Dr. Spock terms a "rather precious possession," the first thing he himself has produced. He may delight in playing with the mess, if his diaper is loose enough and his mother doesn't catch him in time. When she does catch him she tells him, through her whole demeanor, her tone of voice, her very look, that this isn't nice. So he transfers his interest, as he grows, to playing with mud; the consistency is similar but it doesn't smell and it doesn't, usually, offend his mother. Then, Tulane psychiatrist James A. Knight notes in *For the Love of Money,* he moves on to still more socially acceptable spheres, playing with sand, then pebbles, then fruit pits, marbles, buttons and, at last, money —an interesting progression.

Middle-class children learn their lessons well. They know that nice clean money is more acceptable to their parents than any form of messy play and, as a result, they are reluctant to slop around in finger paint. Soiling and smearing, say psychologists who have studied nursery school groups, produce anxiety in middle-class children.

So the preschooler turns to collecting coins instead, anyone's coins. But Jamie's father doesn't like finding his bus fare missing; Ellen's mother is equally annoyed when the change for the paper boy is gone. Both Jamie and Ellen learn to distinguish, very quickly, between pennies and buttons.

They also learn, with astonishing rapidity, that coins are good for something besides collecting. "Allison tugs me to the door every time she hears the Good Humor bell," her mother ruefully reports. "She's only three but she knows she can get ice cream for a quarter." Allison doesn't understand capitalism, free enterprise, the laws of supply and demand, or any theory of economics. She doesn't even understand what a quarter is. She does understand that round, shiny, jingly objects called coins have a magical quality: they can be exchanged for all kinds of yummies, not only ice cream but bubble gum, lollipops, balloons. . . .

And three-year-old Allison in an urban or suburban setting learns this lesson much earlier than her rural counterpart. On a farm, especially that farm of idealized, preindustrial America, there was no ice cream unless it was homemade; certainly there were no tempting bells sounding down neighborhood streets and teaching preschoolers the value of money. There was no ubiquitous TV either, with its never-ending message of, "Ask Mommy to buy. . . ."

Today we, and our children, are irrevocably part of a money society. Television, of course, is everywhere. So, to a lesser extent, is the Good Humor man. Rural children may handle money for themselves later than city youngsters constantly exposed to stores, but they too grow up in a money economy.

The earliest experiences with money are tied in with the toddler's vision of his parents as omnipotent, godlike beings, able to satisfy any whim by producing the coins that turn to treats. And here too we have inescapable emotional ramifications. Comes the day that Daddy first says "No"—and a bolt of lightning splits the child's sky. Daddy is not omnipotent after all; he can't—or worse, he won't—fulfill all desires. Money's long-range emotional significance, according to marketing experts, is enhanced by this early realization that money is one reason the child cannot gratify all his whims. Even in affluent households children are taught not to be wasteful, taught that they can't have everything. "Money doesn't grow on trees, you know." Money comes to be viewed as something with great power; even parents, those mighty creatures, defer to it.

Meanwhile, our preschooler is learning not only that loving parents provide security but that money can be traded for goods. When he buys ice cream, goes to the supermarket with mommy, sees big brother purchase a notebook for school, he learns the uses of money. Later, as the child sees coins exchanged for passage on bus or toll bridge, as they secure entry to swimming pool or movie, he realizes that money also buys intangibles, services as well as goods.

It isn't long before he enjoys shopping for himself, although it may be a while before he fully understands the value of the coins he spends. Sociologist Anselm L. Strauss, in tracing children's comprehension of money, found that even at age five, when most children see that money is necessary to buy things, most still think that "any coin buys anything." It's more a symbol of the transaction than a necessary ingredient. Davey, in his second year of nursery school at the ripe old age of four, understands quite well that you can get milk or bread or candy from the store; he's not quite sure what money has to do with it. "Maybe," he thinks, "the store man needs the money to give to the next mommy."

The more a preschooler is exposed to shopping transactions, the faster his understanding of the uses of money develops. Having older siblings speeds the learning process. "Andrew didn't pay any attention to money until he started school," his father notes. "Now Douglas, at three and a half, sees Andy buying baseball cards and wants money of his own." But, not understanding money or what it can do, a couple of shiny pennies make Douglas very happy, whether he uses them for the supermarket gum machine or tucks them away.

As he grows, however, he will learn to discriminate, to understand the different value of different coins. Most youngsters understand by the time they enter first grade, as Strauss puts it, that "money does not merely accompany each transaction, but in some sense makes them possible." By six and a half, most children can name all the coins, and recognize that nickels buy more candy than pennies, and dimes more than either. But making change, as a rule, is still beyond them; exact amounts must be used. The average child is past eight, Strauss found, before he understands the impersonality of shopping: that storekeepers will sell to anyone, and that the aim is profit.

Today's children may be more sophisticated than the children Strauss surveyed in his classic study of the 1950s; each learning step may occur somewhat earlier, but the pattern of development remains the same. Oklahoma State University marketing professor James U. McNeal studied a group of five-, seven-, and nine-year-olds in the mid-1960s. He found that while fives were generally dependent on parental choices, almost all of the seven-year-olds were shopping by themselves at least occasionally. This generation is more interested in shopping, more concerned with material goods than earlier generations, McNeal writes in *Children As Consumers,* because they handle money earlier, often receiving an allowance by age five, they are encouraged by parents to play the consumer role, they are subjected to child-oriented advertising, they are the object of considerable adult spending and, not least, "they are constantly subjected to the materialistic displays of other children."

A young child gets a much-needed sense of independence from going to the store alone. He gets two levels of satisfaction from shopping: first, the satisfaction every purchaser gets from the object purchased, and second, the "grownupness" of going shopping for himself. That very first trip to the store alone, says McNeal, is "exciting, mysterious and self-rewarding," with a successful errand resulting in a tremendous feeling of accomplishment.

This elation may be the forerunner of all the psychological gratification people of all ages derive from shopping. At a time when things aren't going quite right, at a time when the mood is blue, we all know how comforting it can be to buy ourselves a treat.

For adolescents, individuals in transition, growing up and yet dependent, shopping can be an essential expression of independence. "Seventy-six percent of the teen-agers interviewed," *Newsweek* reported of a 1966 Louis Harris poll, "regarded shopping as one of the experiences they most enjoyed: not so much for what they bought, but for a sense of independence and possession." Lester Rand of the Rand Youth Poll believes that teen-age buying is often motivated by insecurity and serves to satisfy the ego and ease adolescent frustrations.

In the early school years, as in adolescence, shopping is often as much an end in itself as it is a means to an end. The more independence the child has, the more he can achieve socially desirable goals through shopping: he can secure his friends' approval by being free to shop with them as well as through buying the fad of the moment, and he can make himself feel loved and appreciated by buying nice things for himself.

Some are more capable of buying than others, although they may not necessarily enjoy it more. A school psychologist sees a pattern related to birth order: older children spending freely, but carefully, and younger children being dependent and needing support in shopping. "Lorraine has been picking out her own clothes since she turned twelve. She sometimes makes a mistake, buys what I consider (and she sometimes agrees) is a bad choice, but she's pretty careful. She'll go to several stores to find the particular blouse she wants, at a price she thinks is reasonable. Anne is two years younger and anxious to imitate Lorraine. 'I'm thirteen now,' she tells me, 'and I can buy my clothes too.' But what happens is that she'll go shopping and come home empty-handed. Unless I'm with her, or she has some girl friend for company, she's not likely to make a decision."

Economic factors have an impact too, sometimes distorting actual perception. One experiment with ten-year-olds of varying economic backgrounds found that poor children consistently overestimated the physical size of coins, even while looking right at them, a distinction the researchers saw clearly related to the social value of the coins for that child and his family.

But middle-class children, without any particular psychological or economic bias, see coins with their own vision too. Young children, especially, prefer quantity; any three-year-old, says a nursery school director, would much prefer three pennies to one nickel. And there's another more practical problem: "Jeffrey was very perceptive for a four-year-old," his mother thought. "He wanted to know why he could buy more bubble gum with a dime than with a nickel; since the nickel is bigger, it should buy more. He's probably right and we do things backwards."

Compounding this all-too-logical confusion is the small child's understanding—or misunderstanding—of number. "George can count to ten, but he doesn't know how many pennies there are when I show him eight." Parents frequently become irritated by what they see as stubbornness. "If he can count to ten, why on earth can't he put five spoons on the table?"

Once you understand the principles of child development, however, one sees that it isn't stubbornness at all. Rote learning to count, so proudly displayed by many parents, has nothing whatsoever to do with comprehension of quantity. The young child, says Piaget, sees things in very concrete terms; he can count six eggs on the table, but not see that they will fit into six egg cups unless the cups are placed precisely parallel to the eggs. Any variation in alignment, followed by adult demonstration that the numbers do indeed match, is likely to reduce even a very bright five-year-old to frustrated tears. With this very basic inability to conceptualize, to go beyond what is clearly visible, it is not really surprising that the numbers and value attached to coins are difficult to grasp.

Closely related to all of this is the preschooler's view of time. Small children live very much in the here and now, confusing time and place; until they can see the continuity of time and understand it as something abstract yet permanent, they will have difficulty with money. Parents must realize, says Louise Bates Ames, that a child will not truly understand money until he understands time, until he also understands how to share; all of these abstract concepts are interrelated. At the appropriate stage of development, in the primary grades, they all fall into place.

The untamed two-year-old who sees everything as "mine" may be beginning to understand private property; he is not, however, ready to understand the principle of giving and getting in return. Siblings can be a big help here. The only child, who doesn't have to put up with bossy older brothers or pesty younger ones, is at a disadvantage in learning to share, not only possessions but parental attention. He simply doesn't have the same healthy, if aggravating, give and take of family relationships.

Underlying all this, more important than the age at which a given child can tell time, count spoons, share a favorite toy, or see that two nickels make a dime, are the basics of family relationships. Emotional responses to people and things, made up of many factors, are more important in shaping the child's future reactions to money than any lessons about five pennies equaling one nickel.

Does John live in a family where private property is jealously guarded?—"Who took my pencil?" "Stay out of my room." "John, you can't play with Stevie's truck." Or, is the family free and easy with each other's belongings, seeing things as belonging to the family rather than to any one family member? At either extreme, there can be problems. "I could never be sure anything would be where I had left it," recalls one woman. "There was one period, when I was about twelve, when I hated my whole family. I had worked and worked on a project for school, gathering material for a diorama illustrating the signing of the Declaration of Independence. The night I planned to put it all together, I saw that an important photograph was missing; my sister needed it for some project. My mother couldn't understand why I was upset—after all, I had left it out on the desk. I never forgave either my mother or my sister."

Then there's the family where each child has his own pair of scissors and Scotch tape, colored pencils and marking pens, so that each school project is done in isolation, with no give and take, no sharing. Intense possessiveness of this type is characteristic of families newly in the middle class, where having one's own room, toys and possessions is a jealously guarded mark of status. Fortunate the child in the family that takes a middle road, neither too possessive nor too free. "When I need the scissors," a sixteen-year-old says, "I take them from my mother's desk. There's no question but that they are there for the whole family to use—but whoever uses them must put them back so that the next person can find them."

While sharing of possessions can be important in determining emotional outlook toward money, even more important is sharing of the self. Where a parent is often too busy to give full attention to his child, where a mother is overtired or a father involved with other interests—not just occasionally but always—what happens? Apart from the impact of constant inattention on the emotional well-being of both the child and the family, apart from overall mental health, it is very easy to see where the child's possessiveness of a parent, evolving because the parent's attention is hard to secure, can become possessiveness of all the things that connote emotional security. Many a money-grubbing adult, say psychoanalysts, is seeking the parental love he missed as a child.

Even when there's no lack of love and security, money plays a lead role in middle-class consciousness. Unlike the truly rich, who don't have to give it much thought, middle-class parents do have to think about such things as job security, meeting mortgage payments, saving for college. And the children learn a great deal by absorbing parental attitudes; sometimes the lessons they learn are not the lessons parents would teach if they realized they are teaching.

The dinner table, say sociologists, is a more potent educational force than the classroom and is, in fact, the scene where cultural values are transmitted. What kind of values are we transmitting? "The price of eggs has gone up for the third week in a row" might be the complaint of a bored housewife, with nothing to talk about, or it might be a prelude to a heated discussion of the economy, agricultural price supports and where the country is heading. "You should see the Wilsons' new car" may initiate a conversation on what car manufacturers are doing this year—or on how the Wilsons can afford a new car every year. Whichever tack the conversation takes, it often revolves around money.

Priorities come into focus too, more and more so as inflation limits our options. Does the vacation the family wants to take preclude painting the house this year? What if we paint it ourselves? Does it really matter what the neighbors think? Does Sally's mother make her school clothes to save money or to provide a more distinctive wardrobe? Does Sally enjoy wearing these clothes, or would she be happier wearing the same kind of store-bought clothes that the other girls wear?

Even when children are too young to take part in such discussions, they are there, listening, absorbing family attitudes toward money and the things money buys. Families fall into habits of conversation, studies have shown, and dinner-table conversation revolves around similar topics night after night, topics not necessarily reflective of the family's income level, educational attainments, or intellectual interests. The style of talk becomes habitual too. A premium may be placed on wit—or on analytical discussion. Sooner or later, depending on the family's pattern, someone will dissect a neighbor, complain about high prices, or argue politics. If a different subject is brought up by some brave soul, it will be quickly dropped, while the old stand-bys will be probed, analyzed, and talked to death.

It might be a good idea to take advantage of this natural learning period—not to lecture, but to talk about things that really matter. "When I paid attention and I listened to us," a parents says, "I realized there was a good chance our daughter was totally confused about our real values. She probably thinks the things we care most about are that she keep her room clean and that we can paint our house when the neighbors paint theirs."

It isn't only at the dinner table, of course, that the child becomes aware of his family's reactions to money and possessions. When Janie comes in from school commenting on a schoolmate's new dress, what is mother's response? Does mother herself frequently comment on friends' new clothes? Is this a family that notices, and remarks on, tastefully furnished living rooms, well-kept lawns, expensive cars? If so, does good taste or cost determine approval?

The current reduction in American family size, plus the isolation of the nuclear family, has led, among other results, to uncertainty among parents, and constant comparison of their children with others. This comparison leads not only to earlier pressures to walk, talk, and be toilet trained but to conformity in possessions: every tot's toys must be "educational," his clothing at least as good as that of the child next door. This constant comparison, write sociologists James H. S. Bossard and Eleanor Stoker Boll in *The Sociology of Child Development,* creates a tremendous drive for achievement. "From the beginning of his life, the child senses that his place, even in his own family, depends on his achievement and on how he compares with other children. At the same time, he is learning that this is true of his family. On these two levels, child and adult, operates the American pressure to get ahead, by way of both material achievement and social status."

Further pressures arise because children learn early, very early in our society, to compare. Much as parents compare their children, so children compare their parents. "I remember how impressed I was that my friend's father was a lawyer and went to New York every day to an office," a college senior says. "My father had a respectable small business in the community, but it didn't compare." Status is conferred on the children by the occupation of the father. The six-year-old who is the envy of all his friends because his father owns the neighborhood candy store becomes the sixteen-year-old ashamed because his father doesn't do anything "important." Children notice each other's belongings too: "Amy has four pairs of shoes," the six-year-old reports; "Jack's house is enormous," comes from the eleven-year-old. "Our new neighbors are putting in a swimming pool. Can we get one too?"

Most middle-class parents, when they stop to think about it, vociferously deny any intent to make their children super-conscious of possessions. On the other hand, who takes the time to stop and think? Instinctual reactions, based in part on how hard we've worked for our possessions, reveal a great deal.

Here's a multiple choice test: John continues to bounce his ball in the living room after you've asked him several times to stop; in fact, by this time, your voice has risen sufficiently so that his refusal demands action. Before you can take appropriate measures, however, he loses control. The ball ricochets around the room, with several possible results. Quick now, what do you do in each instance?

(1) It hits a table, making a vase wobble, and spilling some water; (2) it hits the baby in his playpen a glancing blow on the side of the head, making him cry; (3) it hits a picture, cracking the glass; (4) it sends a Steuben ashtray, a wedding gift, crashing to the floor; (5) it comes to rest, after some nerve-shattering seconds, with no damage done.

Well, what's your reaction? What bearing does the value of the broken object have on your response? What message are you transmitting about your priorities? "I was horrified," one suburban mother told me, "when I did stop and think, to realize that instead of the respect for property I meant to teach the children, it was coming across as reverence. I got so upset when the ashtray broke that all my verbal lessons about how people are more important than things must have gone down the drain." What's at issue here, of course, is John's original disobedience, disobedience that remains a fact whatever damage is done or not done. Any punishment—obviously there will be punishment—should be unrelated to whether the baby is crying, water spilled, or the treasured Steuben broken—if you can manage to remain that detached, that is.

One burst of anger, of course, doesn't make a pattern. The fundamental question is whether a home is designed to be lived in. Does enjoyment of hard-earned possessions stop at looking at them, short of using them? Do the plastic slipcovers on the white upholstery, removed only for company, reveal a not very well coded message to the children? Are youngsters allowed to play in the living room—or restricted to the "family room?" Where do the adults spend their evenings? Have we reverted to Victorian days when the parlor (living room) was reserved for company and the family sat in the dining room (family room, or den)? In most cases, probably not. Most families in the 1970s seem reasonably relaxed, willing to enjoy what they have. For those who, for one reason or another, are not, a 1946 study bears ample warning: "The middle-class child's discovery that the living-room furniture is more important to his mother than his impulse to crawl over it," writes sociologist Arnold W. Green, "unquestionably finds a place in the background . . . of a certain type of neurosis, however absurd it may appear." Sociological jargon aside, do think twice before putting possessions ahead of people.

At the same time, children must learn a healthy respect for property if they are to grow up civilized. "We didn't want to make Debbie uptight about 'things,' so we childproofed our living room and gave her free rein. But we found we went too far. When we took her visiting she wouldn't keep her hands away from fragile possessions. When it became a choice between not going anywhere and teaching her not to touch, we started teaching. And," Debbie's father concludes, "we're much happier now. I didn't really enjoy a living room that looked like a giant playpen."

Early training, then, conveying our fundamental attitudes toward time, toward people, toward possessions, influences responses to money. Through trial and error most parents, like Debbie's, hit on the proper balance, proper for their own families. We have to be able to live with the attitudes we want to teach, the attitudes that underlie all our specific teaching about the uses of money.

3:

A Talisman for Love

Money, money, money. Security, power, comfort, ease, influence, self-esteem. . . . Money is almost a code word with many levels of meaning—meanings tied in, if things go well, with feelings of well-being or, if things aren't going quite so well, with feelings of insecurity. Position in the community is assured if you have a reliable income; lose that income, through no fault of your own, and your sense of worth is diminished. Millions of Americans, in the Depression years, lost self-respect because of their inability to provide for their families—a situation over which they had absolutely no control. Today status is still defined by adequate financial resources.

Because money is thus linked with personal standing, with self-worth, it has to be important—much more important than its function as an economic tool, as a medium of exchange would suggest. Because it is so important, it becomes entangled with early sensations of love and affection, with positive—and not-so-positive—family relationships. The result: for our children, as well as for ourselves, money becomes a synonym for security and, sometimes, a symbol of love.

Succeeding chapters will describe positive ways of teaching children about money, ways of handling allowances and earnings, spending and saving. Right now let's look at some of the ways money is misused within the family, the ways in which parents—well-meaning and good-intentioned parents—sometimes bribe, reward, and manipulate children. We all do it, sometimes. Some of us do it too often.

There are endless variations. An easy one to see—and perhaps the easiest to alter—is the use of money in direct discipline.

The real class differences in parental expectations lead to the discipline systems that enforce those expectations. Working-class parents, Melvin Kohn demonstrated in his recent studies, value conformity, where middle-class parents try to foster self-direction and inner values in their children. When a child misbehaves, the blue-collar parent reacts to the immediate consequences of his act, the middle-class parent to his intent. (Was it an accident? or did you trip your sister on purpose?) The result: a concern with immediate consequences leads to immediate, usually physical, punishment, quickly over. A concern with intent leads to reasoning, to the implied threat of deprivation of parental love, to arousal of guilt feelings (which may foster the eventual development of a conscience, but which should be handled with care. Too much guilt, especially if linked with money, is counterproductive.)

The two favorite middle-class punishments, teachers and guidance counselors agree, are withholding allowance and keeping the TV screen dark. Seldom related to the misdemeanor, they are simply the easiest things to grab in moments of stress—after the instinct to swat is suppressed by the middle-class parent, brought up to believe that physical discipline, especially if impulsive, is shameful.

We've all heard the monetary applications: "Don't talk to *me* in that tone of voice and expect to get your allowance." "If you leave that garage door open one more time, I'm fining you a quarter." "You forgot to empty the garbage *again*, Michael; no allowance this week." "You broke a glass; you'll have to pay for it."

It may seem logical to insist on replacement of a carelessly broken item, but is it? "After all, I break things too," says a California mother. "We're not that hung up about possessions. You decide whether good things are meant to be used or to be kept. If they're to be used, they may be broken. The choice is between using and not using."

Several issues are raised here, even beyond undue respect for possessions. What actually happens when an expensive lamp goes crashing to the floor, or Great-aunt Mabel's vase is smashed? The child can't possibly replace the lamp, not without mortgaging both allowance and earnings so far into the future that the cause will be long forgotten, his endless lack of money so bitterly resented that any remorse over the accident disappears into its shadow. Then is a symbolic payment worthwhile? He knows that giving up half his allowance, no matter how generous his weekly stipend, can't possibly buy a new lamp. And a prized sentimental possession, such as Great-aunt Mabel's vase, is irreplaceable at any price.

Accepting monetary atonement conveys the distinct impression that you can erase thoughtlessness with cash, buy a clear conscience—and continue to be careless since carelessness is easily paid for. Far better the child's natural and instant regret at the accident—and his parent's evident unhappiness, tempered with understanding that it *was* an accident. "We have a few pieces of china that belonged to my wife's grandmother. We're all careful with them, and I know the children appreciate their sentimental value as much as we do. But we'd rather use them than hide them away in a cupboard, so we take our chances. Our eldest inadvertently cracked a cup one night. He was heartsick. What would have been the point of charging him for it?" Or, as another mother says, "I yell and scream, but I don't charge them. What would that accomplish?"

When parents do charge for misdeeds, says a psychologist who works with young children, money becomes the focal point, not the child and his needs. A system of fines, charging for breakage or withholding an allowance, sets up an artificial situation, one the child can't control. Accidents will happen. Charging for them won't prevent their happening; it only relieves the resultant guilt through the handy medium of money.

Sometimes it's the child's idea. After one thirteen-year-old had a particularly bad week—she knocked over her bedside lamp and smashed the globe; used her mother's electric typewriter and broke the space bar, to the tune of $26 in repairs; dislodged the second hand in her mother's watch so that it floated free; then borrowed her older sister's pearl necklace, and broke it—she sent her little brother with a crumpled ten-dollar bill in hand, "From Annie, toward all the things she broke." "I went upstairs and returned the money," her mother says, "and told her, 'You can't salve your conscience by paying for it. These things happened because you were always dashing, always in a hurry. Money won't change it. You've got to slow down, stop and think what you're doing.'"

Sociologists agree with this mother's instinctive approach. There's a general deterioration of social values, they say, when children are led to believe that wrongdoing can be rectified through money. The development of a conscience depends on the internalization of right and wrong, on the growth of values; it is spurred by remorse at misbehavior, not by paying off the debt through cash.

When a child is fined for misbehavior other than breakage, whether for being rude, snatching the baby's toy, hitting the dog, or leaving the garage door open, there's even less logic. If the child who is rude to Aunt Martha is fined a quarter, does he think politeness has a price tag of twenty-five cents? If he loses his allowance for talking to you in "that" tone of voice, will he be courteous next time?

Few parents really see a connection, a learning link, between fines and behavior, yet we all do it—usually when all else fails. One mother who resorted to fines in an attempt to teach a lesson on neatness quickly realized her mistake. "I got so tired of the kids dumping their coats on the floor," she reports, "that I told them I was charging a penny a coat. The very first time, my son handed me three pennies 'to take care of the next two times.' I had to laugh, but I was defeated before we started." As another mother said, "Sure, I'd fine them—if it would work."

It doesn't work, yet, in desperation, when all our warnings, scoldings, and words of well-meant advice seem to miss the mark, we turn to money—a futile gesture at best since, if the child actually needs the money, he'll get it anyway. "Little is gained," says psychologist Norman Handelman. "Ultimately it all goes back to the child." If he was to purchase sheet music for his flute lesson, you'll have to buy it eventually. If his money was to go for lunch, you're certainly not going to let him go hungry because he left his coat on the floor. It takes a lot more ingenuity—and thoughtful reactions, not instinctive ones—to come up with appropriate punishments, revoking a related privilege, for example, rather than automatically turning to money. But children, too, appreciate the effort. "If you're not mature enough to control your temper, then you're not mature enough to sleep at Janie's house," is more logical than, "If you hit your brother, I won't buy you the dress you want." It's difficult for a child to see the connection in the latter instance (because there really isn't one), and brother may be even more resented.

You do want to discipline a youngster who hits the baby, although your strong disapproval may be enough (kids really do want to please their parents in the long run), but it might be worthwhile to temporarily ignore lesser infractions. Sloppy ten-year-olds frequently grow up to be neat adults—adults who gaze in despair at their own children's sloppiness; maybe if the disorder is kept behind the closed doors of the child's own room, you can live with it.

If you can't, your child can and will learn to obey the household rules. But parents, most parents, do a lot of yelling, a lot of punishing, over issues that are really not crucial. If we could limit the issues to those that really bother us, we might get a better response. Either way, on any issue—whatever you choose to yell and scream about—try to keep money out of it. Bear in mind psychiatrist Lisa Tallal's admonition: "Money taken by an angry parent seems to the child a withholding of love, of approval—and gives money a meaning we really don't mean it to have."

We load money with meaning both because we find security through money and because we need a substitute for the absolute control wielded by the Victorian father but inaccessible to us. With the loss of absolute parental authority in mid-twentieth-century America, parents, sociologist David Riesman writes, try, often unconsciously, to exercise control through manipulation—and children learn to respond in the same manner.

A manipulative tool constantly at hand, too easily misused, is money. As we use it to punish undesirable behavior, so we employ it to reward suitable behavior, to pay for good grades or jobs well done. As money is used this way, it can become a stand-in for human communication, for warmth, approval, and love. While we mean it to be merely an economically useful tool, mean to teach our children to regard it rationally, we often, through our actions if not our words, give it complicating emotional connotations. "When money is used to stimulate performance, a variety of feelings is aroused in the child," psychiatrist James A. Knight writes in *For the Love of Money*. "The money he receives, or fails to receive, symbolizes parental acceptance or rejection, thus assuming unwarranted magnitude."

Children are too vulnerable to be manipulated in this manner, too susceptible to emotional confusion. They should be taught to value achievement for its own rewards. Offering them money instead, psychologists agree, is subversive. Yet parents do, thinking they are teaching the value of work, that they are giving the children a realistic picture of the world.

"We pay the children for all the chores they do around the house, for walking the dog, and for baby-sitting for each other when we go out—if they don't fight. It seems to work." It probably does, on the surface. Yet these children, had parents expected it, would have done all these things anyway. Not joyously, perhaps, at all times—but they're not always ecstatic about doing chores for which they are paid in cash. And they're certainly not developing much sense of responsibility to the family. Unless parents want their children to think of the family as an employer and their place in the family as that of an employee, they should think long and hard about introducing money as a motivational force in all situations. Money distorts family feeling, distorts what should be a relationship based on mutual support.

As pediatric psychologist Lee Salk said emphatically: "I don't believe in using material objects at all as reward or punishment. It's a way of associating feelings of love and acceptance with 'things' and leads some children to desire more and more things, to become acquisitive when they feel unloved or neglected. The child parents call spoiled because he wants things is the child who was given things as a reward for conforming to parents' wishes." And, Dr. Knight points out, money used this way can intensify sibling conflict. If one, getting more things, sees himself as the favored child, the other will feel unloved—"My brother always got what he wanted, all he had to do was ask." And the favored child will feel guilty.

Occasionally, if not overdone, money may play a valid role in stimulating desired behavior. Eight-year-olds, according to Gesell and Ilg in their classic study of child development, like reward systems and respond well to monetary encouragement. Take advantage of this while it lasts, if you like, but be prepared for the nine-year-old's diminishing interest in money as a motivational force. "Laurie would do anything I asked last year, if I offered her some money," her mother mourns. "Now it doesn't make any difference. She won't clean her room for any amount of money." Be glad; Laurie is ready to move on to more mature ways of relating to people.

A Canadian study tested monetary and verbal incentives in middle- and lower-class children. At six there wasn't much difference, at ten and at fifteen there was more, leading the researchers to conclude that middle-class sensitivity to verbal stimuli grows with the child, while lower-class youngsters become increasingly motivated by money. But middle-class youngsters will learn to lean on money too, if that's what we offer in lieu of affectionate approval.

Too many educated parents, anxious to do the right thing, get swept away by whatever is currently fashionable in child rearing. One such fad is "tangible reinforcers" and "behavioral conditioning." But, say psychologists, even if rewards in the form of money and toys seem to foster desired behavior, they are not appropriate for continual use with normal youngsters. They warp desired emotional development. Within the family, the most powerful reinforcers are parental approval and affection.

Children, like adults, appreciate fairness, appreciate knowing what to expect. Surprises are nice, but life shouldn't be consistently unpredictable. When it is, the results can be disastrous, as in this admittedly extreme instance: "Money was arbitrarily given in my family and as arbitrarily taken away," a young woman, a university personnel officer from a western state, recalls bitterly. "There was no logic, just chaos. It was very destructive. I never knew if I was loved or hated, never knew what was going to happen next. I came to distrust money so much that for ten years I would have nothing to do with anyone who had money. Only work paid by the hour seemed trustworthy. And my brothers are just as confused."

Less extreme, but still fundamentally undesirable, is the practice of offering cash inducements for good grades. "We paid our children one dollar for each 'A' they brought home, fifty cents for a 'B'—a 'C' was even up, and they owed me money for 'D's and 'F's. I put it in the past tense," this parent continues, "because we found that one child struggled and struggled to produce C's, while his sister coasted through with no work and got A's and B's. It didn't seem fair and we stopped the payments—which, by the way, didn't noticeably affect their grades."

"My father paid me for good report cards," a twenty-year-old college student told me. "But I would have worked hard anyway. I wanted to go to college." If she hadn't cared enough about college to earn the grades to get there, should she have been spurred on by monetary reward? What would she then get out of college? Or would she have to be spurred further by ever-higher rewards—a sports car, perhaps, or a summer trip to Europe?

"Parents must let a child set his own expectations," adolescent psychiatrist Bernard Yudowitz insists. "If a child earns good grades solely for a reward, or solely to please you, he does not meet his own expectations, his own standards. Don't steal from your child by not allowing him to set his own standards. Then, if your child is angry at you, the easiest and most effective way he can get back at you is by not meeting your expectations, by flunking in school, if that's what would upset you most."

Parents want their children to do well in school; intellectual accomplishment is one avenue of social mobility, an accepted road to success. "My parents always said school was important for the sake of what I learned. But they always seemed to care much more for what my report card said than for what I actually learned. I had one English teacher who wouldn't give anyone short of Hemingway an 'A'—I learned a lot from him, but my parents kept nagging me about the grade."

Because schools often do not encourage parental involvement, written grades may be the only visible measure of scholastic achievement. Parents caught in this bind, unable to see what their children are really doing, press endlessly for good grades—tangible evidence, actually, of test-passing rather than of learning—and then compound the pressure by making money an integral part of the motivation. Psychiatrists say that the self-esteem rightly earned through scholastic success, as through any task well done, is corrupted when the success is spurred by money.

Family relationships, however, are always complex. "We disapprove of giving money for grades," says one mother whose youngsters excel in school, "but my father does it, and it gives him such joy that I can't put a stop to it." Manipulative behavior through money, not a grandfather's harmless indulgence, works both ways. As parents sometimes manipulate children, consciously or unconsciously, through offering material rewards, children can manipulate parents, learning to get what they want by whining and nagging, by evoking guilt. This is often clearly visible in separated families, where children play one parent against the other in monetary terms. One little girl had every request granted by parents eager to outdo each other, to "prove" that, despite their bitterness toward each other, they still loved her. In the end, the objects they gave became valueless for her and she told her therapist, at last, "No one cared enough to say 'no.' " It was easier to give.

The same thing sometimes happens in intact families. Children learn to get from one parent what the other won't give, to stir up guilt feelings when parents deny requests. "I try to keep the children on an allowance," one mother complains, "but my husband always undercuts me by slipping the kids extra money whenever they ask for it." When a child's allowance is constantly augmented in secret by an indulgent parent, Dr. Knight writes, "the child learns to spend all he has, for he is not long in discovering that an empty pocket is sure to bring him more money. Simultaneously, he can punish his parents for not loving him by creating parental anxiety about his rate of spending."

Money acquires emotional connotations early. A small child feels secure in his parent's affection when the parent buys him a treat. He feels rejected when he is refused. There is certainly no reason not to buy treats for our children—and no reason not to reject a request either. It's when parents confuse things with love in their own minds that they feel guilty about denying things to their children; denying things then means denying love while giving things equals giving love. Money itself is never really the issue in these situations; it becomes the symbol, the visible symbol, for parental attention. If a preschooler, for example, jealous of his mother's attention to a newborn rival, is constantly pacified with playthings, instead of with the love and attention he craves, his attachment to material things can become unhealthy.

This doesn't mean, of course, that you shouldn't consider buying the toddler a special box of new crayons so that he can sit beside you drawing while you feed the baby. It does mean that the crayons, or whatever, shouldn't totally replace your attention. Talk to him while he colors and you feed. And keep the same principle in mind with older children. If a nine-year-old is placated with games, or a twelve-year-old with electric racing cars, when what each really wants is a parent to just listen, the pattern of confusing love with material objects is reinforced. "I have treated many adult patients who depended upon objects to gain a feeling of well-being," Dr. Lee Salk writes in *What Every Child Would Like His Parents to Know.* "The objects represented a substitute for love. They constantly engage in looking for things, shopping around, and buying things. Many have reported to me that they feel unfulfilled unless each day they find some *thing* to add to their possessions. The patient's childhood history most often includes the use of objects as rewards for behavior."

A father who constantly distributes gifts and money, says a family therapist, has little sense of what's appropriate for the children; he's too tied up with his own sense of money as power. He uses money as a "buffer zone," she says, to prevent being personally involved with other people. When money is overemphasized this way, its value becomes distorted—and so do the personal relationships for which it substitutes. Unfortunately, children catch on fast and grow up, in such a family, with the belief that material gifts represent love, that if you give a lot you care a lot. As children, they ask for more and more; they want others to buy for them, in a classic case of the "gimmie's" and, when pressed, will meet emotional needs by shopping for themselves. As parents, they think they're showing love by giving things, the more expensive the better. The child who is shown love and approval through money and possessions—*primarily* through money and possessions—is likely to become the individual who accumulates things to combat feelings of rejection—and the adult who perpetuates the cycle with his own children.

Money does have its place. But there's a subtle difference between a bribe and a reward. After five-year-old Brad submitted heroically to having his scalp stitched, when a fall marred a family vacation, his parents let him pick out a present in the toy store; he didn't remove his cowboy holsters for days. But they didn't offer him the gift in advance, as inducement to behave. It's great to say to a child, "Honey, you were very brave at the dentist's today. I know he was rough on you. I'm going to get that record you've been wanting." It's quite another kettle of fish to offer a bribe in advance: "If you're good at the dentist's, I'll buy you a record." The child has to go to the dentist; he's best off learning that life contains such potentially unpleasant moments and that it's possible to cope with them without artificial inducement.

Parents sometimes accidentally fall into these patterns—and find it difficult to get out. "My wife started buying the boys toys every time she took them to the allergist," a computer salesman reports. "They were very little then and it was kind of a payoff for good behavior. They're old enough now—seven and nine—so that we'd like to stop what has turned out to be a very bad habit. The visits are weekly for a good part of the year, the kids have too darn many toys, and, what's worse, they expect to be paid for anything slightly unpleasant. They know now that I won't go along with the game if I take them to the doctor, but when my wife takes them, they rake her over the coals if she protests. It's awfully hard to stop something you've started, but she's got to put her foot down."

When children are ill, it's another story. One active ten-year-old, compelled to spend a summer in bed with rheumatic fever, had the long tedious hours greatly lightened by gifts from his parents and relatives. Most important for Alan, however, more important than the new stamp collection itself, was the time his father spent with him getting it organized. His enthusiasm was spurred by his father's and they spent evening after evening poring over stamps.

Alan recovered and resumed his normally vigorous life. But sometimes children are chronically, permanently ill. "In a children's cancer hospital," reports one physician, "there are so many extremes. Parents are loaded with anxiety and guilt; they are angry at the child for being sick and causing such anguish. They can't admit these feelings, even to themselves. So they bribe and reward the child: 'Be good for this blood test and I'll give you. . . .' These youngsters walk around with pocketsful of money. They don't know what to do with it. It's very sad."

Some of this guilty overreaction, this displacement of emotions onto money, occurs in normal families with normal, healthy children when parents resort to what kids define as bribery. "My father doesn't have to give me money to go bowling just because he wants me out of the house. I'll leave him alone if he asks me to," says a nine-year-old. Children are often surprisingly clear-sighted. "When I was leaving on a business trip," a publisher recalls, "My eight-year-old son asked if I were going to bring back presents. When I said 'yes' and asked both children what they would like, he came back with, 'You're not buying presents for us, you're buying them for you.' And, of course, he was absolutely right."

Not all children can express their preference, not all are as perceptive as the publisher's son. But one member of a parent discussion group remembers her own childhood when she says, emphasizing a different facet of the same problem: "I try to show my kids that I love them, to tell them. My own parents were so busy working to provide us with material things that they never took the time to be affectionate. I wanted that much more than I wanted all the things they gave me."

We all work hard to provide our children with the comforts of life as we all, at least occasionally, bribe them in one way or another. But children's lives—and their feelings about money —are complicated less by what we do (as long as it isn't constant substitution of cash for caring) than by our own uneasiness, our own guilt.

Parents neither can nor should stay home all the time, and there's no need for guilt about absence. When home they neither can nor should spend every moment with the children and, again, there's no need for guilt about inattention (in fact, constant attention would soon prove intolerable for both parents and children).

When parents regularly try to compensate for absence or inattention by slipping the child some extra money, however, it opens up a hornet's nest of problems. As a child may feel absolved from misbehavior by paying a fine, so a parent may thing he has made everything right. But working mothers can't really make up for an empty after-school house through larger allowances; traveling fathers don't fool anyone by dispensing presents every time they return from a trip. "I know what my father is trying to do when he gives me five dollars every time he's away for a few days," a wise sixth grader commented. "I'd rather he stayed home." He can't stay home. But money isn't the answer. Nick would prefer, in fact, an afternoon of his father's exclusive company, much prefer it over several five dollar bills. If the pattern continues over many years, however, he may no longer care. The emotional needs of children simply cannot be met with cash. Attempts to do so give peculiar meanings to money—and to love.

Grandparents can fall into the money trap, too, especially today's swinging grandparents, far too busy for the rocking chair. Sometimes, deciding they've neglected their grandchildren, they, like the compensating parent, offer money as evidence of love. "Here's five dollars. Buy yourself something from me." Sometimes they aren't as direct. "My grandmother wants me to have something 'from her,' she says," a West Coast teen-ager complains, "but she gives my mother the money and tells her to pick it out. That's a cop-out."

Grandparents don't have so much impact on the emotional health of their grandchildren; that burden is left to parents. So a little frivolous financial indulgence is just fine. After all, the accepted grandparental role in our culture is to spoil the grandchildren. But, judging from the comment of the teenager above, some, at least, would prefer personal attention. As with parents, it's the quality of the relationship that counts.

Money distorts relationships, again, when parents resent the sacrifices, necessary or unnecessary, they make for their kids and then, even when they brought the situation upon themselves, inflict that resentment on the children. "We can't take a vacation this summer; your school tuition is going up again," is a remark sure to arouse unwarranted guilt feelings in the child; he didn't, after all, make the decision for private school. Parents do this all the time, says psychiatrist Lisa Tallal, in a very underhanded way. "This is margarine, not butter. Bills were too high this month." The kids listen, feel guilty over what they're costing the family and, sometimes, become more demanding in an unconscious effort to suppress their guilt.

Other parents, not resentful of sacrifices real or imagined, and certainly not intending to make their children guilt-ridden, sometimes unwittingly arouse uncomfortable feelings in the youngsters by references to money. "Don't fix my teeth," a ten-year-old begged, "if it means Andy can't go to camp." Here parents must balance the sharing of decision-making, of financial priorities that help children come to grips with the real world, against the sensitivity that makes some youngsters feel responsible, and guilty, if money is spent on them. They must explain, at times, how financial decisions are reached, that teeth are simply more important than camp, if such a choice must be made. But the explanation should be matter-of-fact. "Children should be made aware that there is not an unlimited amount of money," says Dr. Tallal, "but should not be made to feel guilty for that fact."

Affectionate parents who have good relationships with their children, who try to use money rationally and not overload it with emotional content, occasionally use money unwisely too —or in ways they helplessly view as unwise. "My husband calls it 'guilt money,' " says an editor, "when I take the kids out for a lavish lunch on Saturday because I've been home late three nights in a row, too late to put them to bed. I suppose it is a bribe." But it's not, really. It might be unfortunate if she regularly sent them to lunch or a movie to compensate for her absence; going with them and having a leisurely lunch together, sharing the events of the week, is entirely legitimate.

We are all only human, after all. We will continue to assuage guilt, when we cannot overcome it, by buying a treat. We will continue to demonstrate love by purchasing a present. We may be uneasy, as is the editor, but we should not be. There is nothing wrong with treats; an "unbirthday gift," after all, can be the nicest gift of all.

The point is that children deserve more credit for perception. They see what we are doing if we offer, automatically, to pay them, in one way or another, to get what we want, whether it's peace and quiet around the house or a diminution of the guilt we feel for leaving them. If we are honest with ourselves, and with them, they will understand that sometimes we're too busy, sometimes we can't be home, sometimes we're just too tired to give undivided attention. Children would rather have attention, but they are happy to have gifts as well—gifts that are tokens of our love, not a substitute for it.

4:

Sex and Money, Money and Sex

Females are supposed to be flighty, emotional shoppers, ready to buy a new hat to lift any mood; yet every market researcher knows that men are the true impulse buyers, the shoppers to be lured into the marketplace. Women are supposed to be incapable of doing simple arithmetic, of balancing a checkbook, but actually they manage the books in many families—and are bookkeepers, if not accountants, in many businesses. Yet these pervasive myths affect the way children are taught to manage money. Is there truth to them? Do men and women, boys and girls, handle money differently?

There do seem to be real differences, in our society, in the ways men and women respond to money. But, virtually all observers agree, the differences are culturally determined, the results of conditioned expectations rather than of biological necessity.

Surely there are genetic differences between the sexes. Researchers are still exploring the subtle differences that cause females, for example, to mature more rapidly, physically and intellectually, than males. Girls speak earlier, their perception of the world is sharper, they reach puberty sooner. At six years, writes University of Michigan psychologist Judith Bardwick, girls are about twelve months ahead of boys in developmental age; at nine the gap has widened to eighteen months. Eventually the difference diminishes as growth rate slows down in girls and accelerates in boys, but, as any first-grade teacher can attest, teaching boys and girls together in the early years is a difficult task indeed. Louise Bates Ames argues loud and long, in fact, for later school-entry age for boys, simply because so many six-year-old boys are just not ready for disciplined learning.

Current studies indicate that some behavioral differences may be attributed to prenatal hormonal influences. If this is so, Maggie Scarf writes in *The New York Times Magazine*, then human beings, like some laboratory animals, could be psychosexually neutral at birth, ready to be culturally conditioned. Instead they are, "even before the onset of learning and social experience, 'programmed' or predisposed by early hormonal influences to acquire specific, either masculine or feminine, patterns of behavior." Environmental influences then confirm this basic gender identity.

Eleanor Maccoby, in *The Development of Sex Differences*, notes that identical environmental factors affect boys and girls differently. "The brighter girls," she writes, "tend to be the ones who have not been tied closely to their mothers' apron strings, but have been allowed and encouraged to fend for themselves. The brighter boys, on the other hand, have had high maternal warmth and protection in early childhood." Biologically determined predisposition, then, reinforced by cultural expectations, may (no one quite knows for certain) create the observable behavioral differences between small boys and girls.

But do these developmental differences affect the way human beings respond to money?

In a group of suburban eighth graders the girls demonstrate far more money-awareness than the boys—apparently contradicting the belief that girls are verbally oriented and boys have logical minds, equipped to cope with mathematical and scientific principles. The girls in this group know what a pair of jeans costs, what you can buy with five dollars. They laugh when a male classmate says, "If I had five dollars, I'd buy some jeans, then I'd go bowling, then—" He never gets to finish dreaming, because the girls cut him off. "Girls are more responsible, they're planners," says a banker, mother of two. "Boys live for today, don't give a thought for tomorrow." And a market research executive, whose firm surveys teen-agers, adds: "Girls are always ahead of boys, not only physically but in orientation toward the practical world. Money sense follows logically."

But Harvard psychologist Jerome Kagan does not agree that girls are realistic toward money because they mature faster. "Girls are not more realistic," he says, "just defensive. In our Western culture we reward risk-taking in males, defensiveness in females. Look what happens in the business world. If a male executive takes a gamble, dreams up the Edsel, let's say, and loses, his colleagues will react: 'Good shot, you almost made it.' If a female executive were to embark on the exact same misadventure, her colleagues would say, 'Hey, you screwed up.' We teach females not to fail: be realistic, be conservative, be defensive."

Every society differentiates between the acceptable roles of males and females, anthropologist Margaret Mead has declared. And, in every society, those activities considered unimportant are the activities assigned to women—even if they are economically significant activities which might be reserved to men in another culture.

What does our society expect of males and females?. Males first and foremost, are expected to be aggressive, to go after success. They are oriented toward achievement as a mark of self-esteem—and achievement, in American culture, is usually measured in economic terms. Because money and success mean fulfilled masculinity, money itself becomes a symbol of virile power, along with big houses, expensive cars, boats, and all the other accoutrements of wealth. Unattractive men often become attractive when they have money.

Females, in contrast, are traditionally expected to be passive, dependent, to find gratification through the success of men and not through any achievement of their own. In New Guinea, anthropologist Lynda Ridgeway Cunningham found, some tribal groups assign no names at all to female children. Until marriage each girl is known by her father's name—Johngirl, for example; after marriage, she becomes her husband's—Tomwife. We do something similar, not only in naming (although we grant girls the dignity of individual first names) but, more significantly, in orientation toward the world: a female American child has her status determined by her father; a female American adult has her status defined by her husband. Males, on the other hand, are expected to create their own niche, achieve their own goals and status, starting early in life.

These expectations, of course, exert different pressures on boys and girls. In a study at the University of Minnesota Family Study Center, Irving Tallman has found that boys, measuring their career choices against external success standards, impose constraints on themselves and limit their possible choices. Girls, less subject to family pressures to achieve, are more likely to choose a career on the basis of the quality of life that it offers; they are free to be idealistic. "The norms are against women thinking in terms of money," Columbia University sociologist Cynthia Fuchs Epstein observes. "They think instead of service, of fulfillment." So women frequently go into service careers—social work, teaching, nursing—where the reward lies in interpersonal relationships rather than in money.

Money, the visible symbol of achievement, ranks high among male goals. When *Scholastic Magazine*'s National Institute of Student Opinion asked junior and senior high school students, in February 1973, "Do you think that making a lot of money is, in itself, a worthwhile lifetime goal?" Forty-one percent of the boys said yes. Only 27 percent of the girls agreed. In one study of ninth graders in Georgia public schools there were interesting responses to "Things I Would Like My Child to Have That I Didn't Have." Item One among the boys: Money. Item One for the girls, on a list of five that didn't even include money, is "Friends." Girls, it seems, conditioned not to seek competitive economic success, are brought up to believe that personal human relationships are all-important. If you get along well with people, you succeed—in female terms. And if that is true, you don't, if you're a girl, have to learn how to handle money; the ultimate successful personal relationship, after all, is marriage, in which a woman is supported by a man.

Cultural standards enforce other behavioral expectations which affect the ability to manage money. Because men are expected to achieve, for instance, they must be bold, willing to take risks. Women are expected to conform, to be easily influenced by others. An Oregon Research Institute study analyzed risk-taking in children, by age and by sex, and found that sex differences conforming to cultural stereotypes emerged between nine and eleven: this is when children begin to believe, and act upon the belief, that boys are bolder than girls. Boldness is positively correlated with popularity among boys, as children define the male role in terms of courage, and negatively related for girls. These stereotypes are reinforced by elementary school teachers, mostly women, who expect little girls to be docile and well-behaved, little boys to be noisy breakers of rules, ringleaders in mischief. Later, it's been shown by University of Illinois studies of young couples, men will take risks with money, speculative plunges that unnerve their wives, while women with money to invest opt for conservative choices like savings bonds and bank accounts. It's altogether rational. "After all," one wife remarks, "the stock market can go down as well as up." But, again, as Jerome Kagan sees it, women tend to be defensive when it comes to money, afraid of failure.

Our society also expects males to be producers of economic wealth, providers for the family. Little boys learn early. "You cook dinner," says the chauvinist of the nursery school. "I'm going to work." Females are expected to be spenders of the wealth that men produce, consumers rather than producers in their own right. Because of this basic division men are expected to have greater financial knowledge, to be capable of making intelligent financial decisions, while the helpless little woman is unable to balance the checkbook. "Don't worry about the little woman's mistakes," says the bank ad picturing a check stamped "Rejected: insufficient funds." "Use our overdraft checking and you won't be embarrassed. Her checks can't bounce." At the same time woman in her role as consumer is expected to be a skillful shopper, wisely selecting everything from hamburger to her husband's socks and always, but always, getting the best buy possible. She can stretch the paycheck that she does not understand.

In the organizational world, women volunteers are asked to raise funds over which they will have no control. Men make the decisions. And, when women are in the business world, they rarely exert influence in the financial sphere. They balance the books but have very little voice in allocating major resources.

With the rapid social changes of the 1970s, the movement toward equal rights for all, these societal expectations are changing. But change, change so fundamental that it affects behavioral expectations, is exceedingly slow. Meanwhile many parents, even those who intellectually reject culturally imposed stereotypes, often unwittingly expect different behavior from their sons and daughters—and reinforce the myths about women and money. The influence, in virtually every family, is both overt and subtle.

Conscious distinctions made between boys and girls are easiest to examine. Household chores are frequently assigned by sex. Girls do the dishes, boys rake the lawn, girls dust the living room and, for some reason, boys always take out the garbage. Furthermore, boys frequently get paid when girls do not. "We both did the same chores on the ranch," a college student from Montana says. "My brother got paid; I didn't."

In some families boys always get their allowances from their fathers, girls from their mothers. In others, both boys and girls get lunch and clothing money, basic provisions, from Mother but the allowance, their discretionary spending money, from Father; the money that connotes independence comes from a man.

Sometimes boys are given more money than their sisters. "After all, he needs it more, he'll have to take girls out," one mother explains. "Not only did my brother always get more money than I did," a young woman complains, "he could spend it as he pleased. I always had to account for every penny." Another sex role distinction: boys are expected to be independent, hence they are given independence; girls should be dependent, and they are kept that way.

Because males are expected to be independent they are expected, in turn, to provide for their own needs, to earn money when they need it—which means that in some families they actually are given less money than their sisters. "My father insisted I deliver papers," a college senior recalls. "He said it was good training for the business world, and would never give me movie money. My sister just waited till he was in a good mood, smiled prettily, and got what she wanted." In bringing up girls to be dependent, to rely on men, such fathers unconsciously are teaching their daughters the feminine arts of flattery. It's cute, they think, when a little girl wheedles something from her father; it's not at all cute when a little boy does it. Little girls often demand more, too, says a psychiatrist, always saying "buy me this, buy me that," because they've been shown that love is demonstrated through gifts.

The wheedling that small females learn at their fathers' knees becomes a pattern. Combined with women's supposed lack of achievement drive and "inherent sensitivity" to human relationships, the result can be an unhealthy manipulation of people to get what's wanted, reinforced because straightforward achievement is discouraged in women. One successful business executive, a woman who made it in the years before many companies would hire a woman on management levels, commented: "I've always had to be accommodating, or I was called 'pushy.' My male colleagues could be assertive."

Most women never get to the point of seeing the differences between male and female executives. Many with the ability have been sidetracked along the way by what psychologist Matina Horner, president of Radcliffe, calls woman's fear of success. Boys are brought up to be achievement-oriented, to go out and earn what they want; girls are reared to be attractive to boys, to "catch" a husband—an effort in which the competitive assertion necessary for economic success is a disadvantage. Young women, brighter than boys all through elementary school, suddenly realize that they'd better fall back. By mid-secondary school, certainly by the college years, women students don't do nearly so well as men. Why? Dr. Horner attributes this falling back to real anxiety, a fear of success. In our culture, girls who succeed are in real danger of losing their femininity, insofar as femininity is defined by society's standards. "Don't let the boys know you're smarter than they are," is a classic maternal word of advice.

Even in the early years, when many girls do well in school, some observers claim that the motive is still dependence—girls strive to achieve academic excellence to win the affectionate approval of parents and teachers. Boys, in this view, are motivated by inner standards, by the challenge of mastering a skill, girls solely by the need for approval. If this is so, a fear of failure, of taking risks, is easily understood: if self-esteem depends on approval by others, failure must be avoided at all costs.

Boys are usually given credit for spatial and analytic ability, girls for verbal excellence, although some sociologists feel that these differences, again, may be attributable to social expectation rather than biological distinction. Fourth-grade boys and girls, in one study, proved equally capable of thinking clearly, of solving problems. But the boys were clearly more self-confident, more concerned with power, assertion, competition, and mastery. The girls, as always, were more concerned with adult approval, more apt to settle tensions by conformity.

The stereotypes are firmly in place, however, long before children start school, reinforced by television and the outside world. Even where parents bend over backwards to avoid categorizing their children, the cultural images are pervasive. "My daughter wasn't yet five," a woman attorney says, "when she said she was sorry I wasn't feeling well. I was fine—but she'd decided I must be sick because Daddy was cooking dinner." Even ardent feminists, says one sociologist, find themselves falling into the habits of a lifetime, doing unconsciously what they would not choose to do intellectually. And many parents, their consciousness not aroused, subtly and not-so-subtly perpetuate the old myths.

Girls are more subject to "love-oriented" discipline, to implied threats of withdrawal of affection by their parents, according to Cornell University's Urie Bronfenbrenner. As a result, they are more obedient than boys—and also more anxious, timid, and dependent, fearful of rejection. They are better students, because they are more anxious for the teacher's approval, and they are economically dependent, so unsure of themselves that they need support in making buying decisions. Market surveys confirm that girls are more dependent on others; insecure, cautious and conservative, they examine products carefully. No wonder girls so rarely shop alone. "It's no fun to go by myself," a thirteen-year-old says. "If I have money for a blouse, or want to buy some records, I wait till at least two of my friends can go with me." A gaggle of girls is a familiar shopping center sight.

Because shopping is viewed as a traditionally feminine function in middle-class America, part of the syndrome of woman as consumer, girls are frequently taken along on shopping trips by their mothers and trained in consumerism. But, according to a study of children as consumers by James U. McNeal of Oklahoma State University, independence in shopping is granted to boys earlier than to girls; twice as many five-year-old boys as girls in this study were going to stores and shopping on their own. What results, then, is knowledgeable consumerism on the part of girls (knowing what a pair of jeans costs), which is good, but its corollary, not so good, is conformity, dependence on the opinions of parents and of peers. Forty percent of the seven- and nine-year-old boys in the McNeal study, and 60 percent of the girls, reported that their purchases were influenced by their friends—and that they, in turn, influenced their friend's buying decisions.

The major influence, on both boys and girls, is parental attitudes toward money. Conflict, of course, makes an impression. But so do basic patterns of money management, casually adopted and casually accepted: who doles out money to whom, who writes the checks and balances the checkbook, who decides what to buy and when.

Children pick up a variety of messages from the way money is handled within the family. They learn, from parental attitudes, that women should work, or shouldn't, that earnings should be pooled, or not, that decisions to spend are made jointly, or independently, just as they learn that money is to be spent or hoarded, budgeted or frittered frivolously away.

Sometimes they learn that he who brings in the money controls the purse strings, and the family. "My father gives my mother a household allowance each week," a teen-ager notes. "If she needs more, she has to ask for it." In these families children are unlikely to view marriage as an equal partnership. Where there is "his" and "her" money in the family, says one psychologist, children are unlikely to see their own position in the family as of equal value, equal importance, whether boy or girl. And, according to sociologists, the traditional docility of women, their economic dependence, is a strong if invisible socializing influence on their children.

In other families all the income is family income, no matter who actually earns it, and the children see common funds used to meet common goals. "My folks stick all the money in a drawer, and they take what they need when they need it." When money is shared openly, status isn't defined by sex.

Women, whether they earn or not, are frequently in charge of day-to-day family accounting, especially, says one banker, in upper-middle-class families. Bill-paying has become an onerous housekeeping chore instead of a symbol of financial responsibility, a task men now shun instead of proudly assume. So women write the checks, balance the checkbook, and keep track of the family's solvency. Children accept this as a feminine function.

But writing the checks is an economically insignificant task; it does not necessarily entail financial responsibility. "My mother writes all the checks," one youngster observes, "but she always seems to ask my father if it's all right to buy a new dress." The treasurer of a corporation does not decide where to spend the money. There's an old joke that has a man saying: "I make all the big decisions, my wife makes the little ones. I decide whether the President is right or wrong, whether our foreign policy makes sense or not; she decides where we go on our vacation, what kind of car to buy, and when to paint our house." The joke rings a sour note for many women. In actuality, they may pick out their husband's socks but they wouldn't dare make a major purchase without his approval. Some women draw a mental line. "I'll spend thirty or forty dollars on a dress if I'm shopping for myself," a teacher says. "But I only buy expensive clothes if my husband is along."

Children know where the real center of power is. They don't have to be told. "My father came home with a new slide projector and my mother got mad because he didn't tell her he was going to buy one," reports an eleven-year-old. "She never buys big things like that." Competition between husband and wife is often expressed through money, that ubiquitous symbol of power. "I bought myself an African sculpture I'd been wanting, but didn't think we could afford," says one woman, "when my husband went out and bought himself an expensive camera."

A lot depends on the funding of the account, says a banker, literally and psychologically. Does the husband put his whole paycheck into a joint checking account on which both can draw? Or does the husband allocate part of his income to household expenses, and give a weekly allowance to his wife? If he does so distribute the funds, is the amount determined jointly, on the basis of need, or arbitrarily, depending on what he thinks things should cost? Arbitrary decisions invariably invite resentment. Husbands may be as ignorant of the costs of running a household as parents are of the cost of model airplanes. Both wives and children resent such ignorance on the part of people who insist on controlling the purse strings. And wives, especially, resent being treated like children.

But the patterns seem to be changing among young marrieds. There's a conscious effort today on the part of young people to work out different styles of marriage, less centered on who earns more. Even without conscious effort, there is change. Fewer husbands retain absolute authority. Robert Ferber of the University of Illinois Survey Research Laboratory has found in an ongoing long-range study that family financial management, starting out as a joint venture between bride and groom, frequently shifts by the end of the second year of marriage. By this time, he finds, fewer than half are still a joint venture, one-quarter of the husbands have assumed control, and slightly more than one-third of the wives have taken over as what Ferber calls Family Financial Officer, not only carrying the primary responsibility for paying bills but making and executing decisions, keeping track of expenditures in relation to budgets, allocating surplus cash. "We were going to decide everything together," says one young wife, "but it just got to be too cumbersome. Now we each buy what we want or need for ourselves and just consult when it comes to something major like a new car. I wound up writing all the checks and knowing more about our financial affairs than Bob does because he simply can't be bothered. We'd wind up in a lot of trouble if I left bill-paying to him—but I must admit that makes me mad sometimes."

More and more of these young wives are working. Women who earn feel freer to discuss how the family's money should be spent. "I need a new winter coat" becomes less a subject for negotiation when the person who needs the coat also earns money that can pay for it. Women who earn are more likely to see themselves as people, not just instruments for the care of home and family. Wives of blue-collar workers, too, are finding this kind of independence attractive, according to a 1973 study by Social Research Incorporated. They, like middle-class women, are no longer as content to stay at home, docile and dependent.

But few things change more slowly than attitudes. Older women, upper-middle-class women who do not need to work, are less likely to do so. And many men, especially the generation that reached manhood during the Depression years, did not and do not want their wives to work. Sometimes the wives listen; sometimes they do not. "There was a huge fight in my house when my mother wanted to get a job," a man now in his thirties recalls, "even though we certainly could use the money. She did work, finally, but my father always decided how the money was spent, all the money." Being able to provide for his family made a man a man; if he did not in fact provide the total income, he would at least control its spending.

This traditional autonomy for men is a tradition that dies hard. Men spend freely, says Lora Liss, a Fairleigh Dickinson University sociologist. They always have, because they earn the money. When women earn and pool their earnings with their husbands', the men continue to exercise autonomy, to spend freely. The women continue to seek direction, to depend on their husbands. No matter how much she earns, he often remains the financial decision-maker, the holder of power. Says one woman: "I feel much better now that I'm working—but I still asked Phil if we could manage a new coat for me this year."

Today, in a trend that may change these traditional attitudes, far more women are working and far more young women expect to work. Money is a factor, but so is achievement, the goal of individual success. Recent studies by the Institute of Life Insurance demonstrate a dramatic shift in expectations: in 1970 the young women surveyed still anticipated, on the whole, marriage and husbandly support; in 1972 they looked forward to financial independence.

There are contradictions, however. A 1973 study of college freshmen, men and women, by the American Council of Education found that only 30.4 percent agreed that the activities of married women are best confined to home and family; three years earlier the figure was 47.8 percent. Yet, although today's young men may intellectually accept the fact that their wives will work, on-campus interviews with college students, supposedly in the vanguard of social change, show that emotionally they still prefer the old clear-cut role division: women stay home and care for the children while men work, women consume what men provide. At least this is the pattern they foresee for their own families-to-be.

Even men who accept that their wives want and need to work often begin to feel threatened if and when their wives earn as much or more than they do. Marriages have foundered, according to psychiatrists, because husbands simply could not accept financial equality. Although rarely expressed—the "cause" of breakup is usually something else—such men find their virility, their essential masculinity, threatened by their wives' success. It takes a secure man to accept a woman as his equal. And men socialized from infancy to consider economic success the true measure of a man have difficulty being psychologically secure enough to share that success.

Wives themselves have tended to regard their earnings as supplemental, even when substantial. "My husband pays all the bills," says a college professor. "My income goes for little things that please me." When women don't take themselves or their earnings seriously, it perpetuates second-class status. And the children of "pin-money" mothers grow up to regard women's work as more avocation than vocation, more hobby than career. All the equal pay for equal work, all the doors battered down in the name of equal rights, won't help if both boys and girls don't grow up to take women's work seriously.

Many women, of course, are very serious. Many men take their wives' earnings and career goals seriously. Unthreatened by their wives' economic independence, secure in their own masculinity, they are very encouraging. "I can support us," says an attorney. "But my wife is much happier when she's working. And it gives us both that much more money to draw on—there's no denying that it raises our standard of living." Greater income means more freedom for the whole family: husband, wife, children.

The argument that the children of working mothers are somehow disadvantaged has been laid to rest by now, not only by theorists of the feminist movement but by ample sociological research. We know now that children thrive on quality, not quantity of care, that many women are better mothers when they are not hovering twenty-four hours a day, so wrapped up in their children that they have no life of their own. Betty Friedan pointed out recently that women who've been brought up in an atmosphere where achievement is highly regarded, and then are kept from personal achievement, focus their goals, their striving and competitiveness on their children.

Interestingly, even when women work, children view the woman's role as essentially domestic, the man's as provider. This finding, disturbing to fervent feminists, reassures sociologists who feel that children are not confused in sex-role identity because their mothers work. Daughters, in at least one study, also seem to have more sense of self-worth when their mothers work; they thought their fathers as well as their mothers might actually prefer having daughters. Either way, the example of a working mother prepares a girl more realistically for the world we live in, a world where married women are very likely to remain in the labor force throughout maturity. It also shows children, both boys and girls, that women can manage money.

Not all women work, of course, and not all women will work. Women should not be forced to work, any more than they should be forced to stay home. But non-working wives should see themselves as full partners in marriage, sharing financial decision-making for the good of the family. If they need reinforcement they must know that it would cost their husbands thousands and thousands of dollars a year to replace their services, those services as housekeeper, cook, laundress, and supervisor of children that they, their husbands, and their children take for granted. A study by the College of Human Ecology at Cornell University has measured the dollar value of household work. The annual input of housewives, women not employed outside the home, ranges from $4,700 to $9,400, depending on the number and ages of their children. But stay-at-home women, no matter how well-educated, too often downgrade themselves. "I don't do anything," says a college graduate, "I'm just a housewife." Occupation: none. What do the children of these mothers absorb about the role of women and the importance of money? Are only activities remunerated in hard currency worth anything?

The primary historical rationale for marriage has been an economic exchange: sexuality for support. Legally, through the centuries, a wife had no standing; under English law she actually lost her individual existence at the altar, becoming legally inseparable from her husband. She could not own property, enter into contracts, sue or be sued. American law, derived from this English foundation, designates the husband as head and master of the family. Although married women in this country can now own property and sign contracts, husbands, in most states, retain the obligation to support wife and family. Although this is changing, gradually, as equality takes hold, the psychological impact has been substantial. While happily married women have had a great sense of security, women in general have had little self-confidence—and a known inability, at least in theory, to manage money. Society in general has suffered, in consequence, the loss of an otherwise productive group of citizens.

When women have entered the job market, they have faced consistent discrimination. Why hire a woman, when men need the jobs to support their families? Why pay a woman as much for the same job?—she doesn't need the money.

Although some of the legal barriers are down in the mid-1970s, the psychological barriers remain. Women are still not represented in as many occupational classifications as men. Women still often do not receive equal pay for equal work; despite federal law to this effect, job titles often mask discrimination. And women still, all too often, cannot receive consumer credit on the same basis as men. Women's earnings are often discounted when couples apply for a mortgage. And women earning substantial salaries frequently are denied the same line of credit a man of equal income would receive. The cases can be endlessly documented. But, in toto, they reinforce all the myths about women and money, and have a horrifying effect on the way our children grow up to view money and the power that money brings.

For money is power. There is no deep psychological significance to this simple fact, no need to look at money masquerading as masculinity, although at times it does. Money gives people, men and women, the ability to control their lives. When they have money, therefore, they must know how to handle it; boys and girls alike need to be taught the basic skills of money management. Whether girls grow up to be traditional housewives, responsible for the family budget, or liberated career women, responsible for their own livelihood, or a combination of both, they need to know how to budget and shop, earn and save, invest and plan for the future.

Patterns are changing. Some brave souls are trying new forms of marriage, new approaches that stress sharing. A few couples, embracing new life-styles, have gone so far as to keep all their money separate, each contributing a fixed share toward household expenses. This is rare, and likely to continue to be so. But Robert Ferber, in his Illinois studies of ordinary couples, found that the usual husband-wife roles are shifting, that wives have taken on a more dominant role in planning the couple's life-style and in handling their finances. The whole notion of women as dependent is changing, says a psychoanalyst, as women assume a closer to equal share of responsibility for the family.

As more women work, more women will feel freer to share in financial decision-making, to share the power that money represents in the family. More nonemployed women will recognize the value of their contribution to family well-being —and demand a share in financial responsibility as well. Their children, the children of both employed and nonemployed women, will grow up in the realization that people, male or female, can handle money. They will grow up knowing that women can and do work, and that whether or not they hold down outside paying jobs they are still equal partners in marriage, in decision-making. Their children will grow up, boys and girls alike, expecting to fulfill themselves as human beings, through work and through family. Then, perhaps, the myths will be dispelled.

5:

Making Allowances

All children, without exception, benefit from the experience of actually handling money for themselves. Outgoing or shy, temperamentally expansive or emotionally conservative, it doesn't matter: using money is the only way to learn the financial facts of life.

Since few youngsters have much opportunity to earn before they are teens, the money used for these practice sessions must come, in one way or another, from the family. Practice sessions? Yes. You can't learn to play tennis without a tennis racket; you can't learn to read without books; you can't learn how to handle money if you never touch the stuff.

Children come in contact with money in many ways: helping to select a birthday gift, running to the store for the horseradish mother forgot, taking cookie money to school. But they learn most effectively with an allowance, with regular pocket money to be managed, or mismanaged, by the child himself.

Children differ enormously in their sophistication about money, of course, as they do in everything else. "I'm going to make lots of money when I grow up," Scott says fervently. "I'm going to be rich." Yet his mother finds his birthday money lying on the dining room table, where it remains until she puts it away. Scott's kindergarten classmate doesn't express grandiose long-range goals but sees money in more concrete, immediate terms; Michael relishes a shopping trip to the dime store, where it takes him three-quarters of an hour to decide to buy an owl-shaped eraser. One six-year-old pesters his parents for an allowance; the next has no idea what to do with money he's given.

And parents differ enormously too. Some start an allowance without being asked. Others don't think children should have spending money until they're ten or twelve; still others think all money should be earned. And there are those who prefer to dole out money for each expenditure rather than give the kids a set amount on a regular basis. It seems to have little to do with family income and almost as little to do with how the parents themselves manage money.

One couple, conservative in their spending, habitually records every penny. Yet they give their children weekly allowances. Other parents, keeping equally meticulous household accounts, will have no part of allowances: "It's a waste of money." People who don't budget at all think their children should learn to live within an allowance. Others, impulse-buyers to the end, won't give allowances: "We can't keep track of specific amounts—how can we ask the children to?"

A salesman earning a substantial, if erratic, living from commissions, sits in the den of his $80,000 Long Island home and asks, in total bewilderment, "We give them everything they want. What would be the point of an allowance?" He might be interested in a young woman, deeply in debt and blaming her woes on overly permissive parents: "They never taught me to put a limit, to live within an income. I've always bought whatever I wanted, and I still do."

Some parents have well-considered reasons for refusing allowances. "I don't like the idea of their blowing money in the candy store," one father says. "I'd rather they ask me when they have something specific to buy. Then I can approve or disapprove." "You don't get something for nothing in this life," a schoolteacher declares. "They might as well learn now that you don't get money without working for it. When they want it badly enough they'll earn it."

Both parents have a point, but both points can be countered. True, it's easier to control expenditures—and the child—when you pass judgment on each purchase. "My mother never gave me an allowance," an accountant recalls. "She said if I needed money to ask her. I resented having to ask her, resented her having to approve every purchase. I still resent her attempts to control me." Such close supervision by parents, one study found, does reduce spending mistakes—as it reduces, too, the sense of responsibility felt by children. It also places money at the core of parent-child relationships.

True, children learn more about the value of money by working for it. But young children, seldom able to earn, still need money. By the time they are old enough to find work, they may have learned, instead, to manipulate their parents to get what they want. "I never had an allowance," a successful businesswoman recalls. "I didn't want one. It was much more profitable to talk my father into giving me money, or buying me what I wanted. I'm sure I came out ahead." Or, as a sixth grader reports, "I don't want an allowance. I get more money without one than my friends do with one." No doubt: many parents have found that cash outlay diminishes when the children go on fixed amounts. Money doesn't dribble away. And, more important, there's less nagging, whining, and wheedling, less playing on moods and emotions.

Children often prefer fixed amounts, too, even if they get more the other way. They like to know where they stand. "My parents were irrational about money," a young woman vividly recalls. "I would get a bucket of money dumped on me, then nothing. I always wanted money of my own, no matter how little, that I could count on."

"Material things come too easy with an allowance," a mother insists, "and competition starts too soon." But American middle-class parents are dedicated to providing the best for their children; in the process they unquestioningly spend enormous amounts. If the dollar outflow for piano lessons, ice-skating, bowling leagues, Scouts, summer camps, movies is not begrudged—we're not even talking now about the food and clothing children consume in endless quantities—why is it so difficult to let children have money to spend on themselves? Why is it more materialistic if *they* spend it than if *we* spend it?

Yet there are enormous emotional hangups involved in adult responses to money, hangups that make it difficult to be rational with our children, to treat money with objectivity. Some people would joyfully give their children anything in the world, anything at all—except money. "Some husbands control their wives with money," says psychiatrist Lisa Tallal, "and some parents control their children." Such parents may say the children will waste it, they may say the children don't need it—actually, money symbolizes such power to these people that they cannot share it with their children. They cannot re-linquish control, emotionally or monetarily, and give a child the chance to grow, to exercise his own judgment and profit from his own mistakes.

Parents who do give allowances are trying to give their children a degree of independence; in doing so, they are backed by most child-development specialists. After all, if money is a tool in our society, which it is, the only way to learn to use it is by doing so. Opportunities to spend money doled out by parents for specific purposes are not opportunities to make decisions, to plan ahead, to determine value, to make mistakes or be responsible. In any event, says one parent, "It's beyond the wisdom of Solomon to pass judgment intelligently on each request, even when I'm not under pressure."

Regular spending money, then, is a preferable way to meet the child's needs, both his practical need for money and his emotional need for independence. But what about the mechanics of it all? When should it start? What should it include? Should it be linked with behavior, grades, or chores?

When a toddler wants to buy something every time he's with

you in a store, when a preschooler begs for pennies because his older brother has money in his pocket, when a first grader regularly passes stores going to and from school—any or all of these circumstances might prompt you to start thinking about providing pocket money. Very small children don't have much real need for money, though, and can't be expected to exercise much judgment. Any allowance at this age should be small change, just to introduce them to the idea of money—or just to ease the pressure to buy ice cream every day or a token in every store. Because a preschooler's concept of time is so vague, too, it needn't be given at regular intervals, but as occasion demands. "I give Joanna a dime when we go to the five and ten. She knows she can spend it and when it's gone she gets no more. If I happen to be there twice in one week, she'll get it twice; more likely it's once or twice a month."

Before long, though, the allowance should go on a regular basis and be an amount that relates realistically to the child's needs. Make it weekly, at least through elementary school. It's easiest for parents to remember a specified day, and a week is a manageable unit for the child. By the time youngsters reach high school they should be ready to budget on a monthly basis.

What's important is consistency. "My mother always forgets, or she's 'too tired' and can't be bothered," a youngster complains—and his classmates nod in sympathy, clearly familiar with the problem. If you agree to give an allowance on Saturday, give it on Saturday if at all possible. A businesslike allowance, given in a businesslike way, teaches the best possible lessons about money. If you can't give it for some valid reason, the child is entitled to an explanation. It doesn't make much difference which day you choose, as long as you stick to it —although at least one parent noted a preference for Sunday "because the stores are closed and he has to stop and think before he runs off to spend it all."

The definition of an adequate amount poses more than a few problems and, indeed, sometimes becomes an insurmountable stumbling block. "We have never been able to decide what items should be included in a reasonable allowance—or for that matter what is reasonable—so, depending on cash on hand," one mother reports, "we deal with individual requests." But there is a solution, achieved by sitting down, with the children, and talking about it. "We schedule a talkfest at the beginning of each school year and discuss the children's financial needs. Then we decide which ones they can manage, and which we should continue to fund separately. Each year," this father says, "the kids seem capable of handling more of the necessary outlay."

Start small. The needs of a first or second grader are few—a comic book, a "special" eraser, baseball cards when all his friends are collecting—and he shouldn't be given the responsibility for keeping large sums. If the child joins Cub Scouts or Brownies, the allowance could reasonably include the dues, plus a small amount for the social necessities of a young child's life. But even at this stage, parents must face the fact that inflation has had an impact; the cheapest comic book has gone from fifteen to twenty cents and there's no such thing as a ten-cent candy bar. "I thought my six-year-old would be pleased to have a dime of her own each week," a parent ruefully notes, "until she made me realize that there's absolutely nothing you can buy with a dime that's worth having."

Most allowance-givers seem to have recognized these inflationary facts. A 1972 survey by *Money Magazine* revealed median allowances of twenty-five cents for youngsters under seven (a good sum with which to start, replacing the now valueless nickel of yesteryear), fifty cents for eight- and nine-year-olds, a dollar for ten- through thirteen-year-olds, and two dollars and fifty cents for fourteens and fifteens. But the range was very wide: children seven and under received from twenty cents to two dollars and fifty cents, teen-agers of fourteen and fifteen, from seventy-five cents to ten dollars. Southern parents, in this survey, were the most tight-fisted, midwesterners most generous, a finding that may reflect regional price differentials as much as it reflects any basic philosophy.

Averages are, at best, only guidelines. Each family must consider the specific needs of each individual child. And, as any child grows, so grow his financial needs. More and more is spent each succeeding year on behalf of the school-age child, whether it's spent by the child himself or by his parents. Parents have to determine, as the youngster moves into fourth, fifth, sixth grade, just how much of this outlay he can be expected to manage—and whether these regular expenditures should be treated as part of the allowance. One family permits a child to pay for her flute lessons; another questions whether bus fare should be dispensed as a lump sum. The argument *for* is that children learn to budget by handling large sums, including both fixed and discretionary amounts; the argument *against* is that nothing is gained by making the child a conduit for money over which he has no control.

But the biggest bone of contention seems to be lunch money. The family that includes it in weekly allowance is, in effect, providing a bonus when there's a school holiday. Parents who allocate it separately frequently wind up irritated at the necessary calculations each time the school week fluctuates. One mother doesn't mind her ninth grader taking lunch from home and spending his lunch money on something else; another child has to return the money if he decides to pack a lunch. Some youngsters simply can't handle large sums. "If Peter gets all his money at once, he'll go out and buy an airplane model. Then he either borrows from his friends at lunchtime, which we don't like, or he doesn't eat, which is worse. We've had to go back to giving him money for lunch each day." It gets very complicated.

So does the subject of recreation. One family provides the necessary funds, independent of allowance, when their twelve-year-old signs up for a community bowling league, but expect his allowance to cover occasional bowling with his friends. It's a matter of mobility too. "When we take the children to the movies, we pay. When they go by themselves, they pay."

Either way, the money adds up. "We thought a dollar a week was a generous allowance for an eleven-year-old," a California mother said. "Then we realized we were following the allowance, each Saturday morning, with another dollar for the movies or two dollars to go ice-skating. It just didn't make sense and we had to wrestle with whether to give her the money all at once and let her allocate it. We haven't yet been able to decide, mainly because it seems, in principle, so out of line to give an eleven-year-old three or four dollars a week." One Connecticut mother, who gives her thirteen-year-old five dollars a week free and clear, chalks it up to independence. "She's got to be able to decide, for herself, whether she wants to go bowling or ice-skating in a given week. If she had to come to me for the money each time, she'd also have to discuss the decision."

The amounts that loom so large bring us back, inevitably, to inflation. It would have been out of line for our parents to give us three or four dollars a week in those long-ago years when we were eleven, or five dollars at thirteen—but the dollar, and what it could buy, was vastly different then. If an under-twelve can go to a movie for a dollar, and you permit a movie weekly or every other week, then the child must have money enough, not only for the movie but for transportation, if necessary, and a box of popcorn, as well as for an occasional treat in between movies. The ante ups sharply when the watershed of twelve is left behind and the child, at least to ticket-takers, becomes an adult.

To some extent, even where parents are determined not to succumb to community pressure, the amount of money a child needs is related to what's available in a given community and what his friends are doing. If all of John's buddies are off to the roller-skating rink, he's not going to be consoled by a maternal suggestion that he go sledding.

It's extremely important for elementary-age children to fit in comfortably with a peer group. Six- to twelve-year-olds are beginning to develop a very necessary independence from their parents; if their parents won't let go, tremendous conflict and, sometimes, lasting dependency, results. Of course, six-year-olds don't get the same kind of independence, nor can they handle it as twelve-year-olds, but they too need to get along well with other children. Part of getting along well is being able to do things together. And, while many activities are free, all too many are not.

Some children have earlier opportunities to spend than others. In densely populated urban areas youngsters frequently pass many stores on the way to school; suburban children may pass nothing but row after row of houses. The urban child gets about on his own more readily, while the suburban child, like his parents, frequently requires wheeled transportation. On the other hand, some urban children, these days, are so sheltered that they don't go to stores alone either, to movies or to bowling alleys. "We just let our eleven-year-old daughter go to the store alone for the first time, with great trepidation," a Manhattan mother reports. "So she's had no chance to develop any money-awareness."

Both mobility and exposure to temptation play a part in determining how much money a child actually needs. A seven-year-old who walks to school, comes home for lunch, and never passes any stores can't make the same use of money as a ten-year-old who needs bus fare, lunch money, Scout dues, and a little extra for the ice cream truck that parks next to the schoolyard. That's obvious. What isn't so obvious is the remaining question: Do you include bus fare and lunch money and Scout dues in a weekly allowance—which may then total five or six dollars without much discretionary spending power—and tell a fifth grader to budget it? Or do you handle each amount separately, doling it out as required?

Both maturity and temperament play a part in the answer. The child who leaves his money lying on the table and his coat on the floor, who tends to be generally forgetful, may best have his money handled for him. If Peter insists on buying airplane models instead of lunch, he's not ready to budget his lunch money. There's little point, with such a youngster, in opening the door to the inevitable recriminations when he loses his money, misspends it, or runs out too soon. His age has nothing to do with it.

A capable child, of the same age as his forgetful friend, responsible in his school work and in caring for his personal needs, can reasonably be expected to take care of his lunch money from a weekly sum, although there's no need to burden him with everything at once. Gradually increasing the responsibility, while meeting each child's individual needs, works best for most families.

But meeting each child's individual needs, a desirable goal in theory, does raise certain problems, notably that of siblings. "My sister gets the same amount I do and she's two years younger," a thirteen-year-old complains. "It's not fair." Second children often get an allowance earlier than first; they're more money-conscious and more likely to ask for one, and parents are already accustomed to the idea. But should the amount be parallel? It's a sticky question. With inflation taking its toll each year, it's easy to have a seven-year-old needing much more than her older brother did when he was seven. But his needs have probably increased too.

If you agree that an allowance should reflect needs, you probably don't tie it too closely to age. "Susan is far more social at eleven than Carol was," their mother notes. "She needs much more money to keep up with her gang of friends." Which brings us back to differing temperaments. The bookworm whose joy in life is reading and the extrovert who spends every minute playing ball don't have much need for money. The quiet child who loves to paint, and needs supplies, the collector, the ice-skating enthusiast, are children of a different type, with far more need for ready cash. You have to take these differing needs into consideration—but draw the line carefully when siblings are involved. It isn't really fair to penalize a child financially because he enjoys reading, while his social-butterfly sister reaps the rewards.

Another interesting question with respect to siblings is raised by family relations authority Richard H. Klemer, who suggests that parents ought to encourage pooling of allowances more than they do, to encourage cooperation. "My kids get together and buy us an anniversary present," one parent observes, "but otherwise it's completely to each his own." Most parents, allocating allowances, as they should, to meet each child's specific needs, simply don't think of urging them to share. Yet, says Klemer, to insist on separate accounts fosters selfishness, an attitude that can have unfortunate consequences when the children grow up and marry.

Parents who are flexible sometimes, if accidentally, come up with workable solutions. "When Evan asked for extra lunch money for extra desserts (his lunch money is separate from his allowance), we decided after consultation to increase his allowance fifty cents a week instead, giving him ten cents a day for the extra sweets he seemed to crave. Interestingly," Evan's father goes on, "we found that he's not buying desserts very often. Instead he buys a magazine, or saves up for an extra session at the skating rink." Evan's parents, wisely, don't object; setting priorities, deciding how to spend limited funds to derive the most satisfaction, is an important part of growing up—and people who don't learn this lesson early are the ones who wind up overextended as adults.

But Evan's parents do eliminate his allowance altogether if the family is on a vacation trip: "We're taking care of all his needs then, he has no need for money." Some parents see it differently. "We prefer Danny to buy his souvenirs without asking our approval. I would find it hard to approve an over-priced deck of cards just because it has a picture of Niagara Falls on the back, or the made-in-Japan plastic 'Indian' jewelry he once bought. But if it's his money, he's entitled to make his own selections. After buying junk a couple of times, he learns."

When children go away to summer camp, and spending money is deposited for them in the camp bank (often, at the camp's suggestion, in amounts far in excess of their pocket money at home), most parents suspend the allowance. When a child stays home during the summer, some families curtail the allowance on the theory that he doesn't need it as much or in the expectation that he can earn some money if he really wants to. Others, in the same community, will increase the allowance for the summer because "they need money if they're going to be able to do anything." And many keep the youngster's finances on an even keel all year round. There's no easy answer to this one; each family has to take each situation as it comes.

Whichever needs you decide your child can handle, whether all-year-round or during the school term, be sure to include a discretionary amount as well. An allowance that is totally allocated before the child touches it is not an allowance at all, and not a learning tool. It may be convenient for you to give the child the money you want him to put into the collection plate each week, but don't call it his allowance and imply that it's his to spend if in fact it's not. Think about it: If you give the child fifty cents and then require that he put twenty-five cents in his bank and ten cents in the collection plate, what has he got left? Can he do anything with fifteen cents? Learn anything about what it's possible to do with money?

At any age, too little money makes an allowance meaningless. Whether it's the eight-year-old with fifteen cents or the eighth grader with a dollar, the allowance that doesn't permit a youngster to keep up with his friends and participate in community activities is worse than no allowance at all. It's just a source of endless frustration for the child and, inevitably, conflict for the family.

In order for the allowance, the discretionary part of it, not to be unreasonably small, parents have to make some effort to know what things cost—the things near and dear to their children's hearts. "My parents have no idea," says one eighth grader. "They think I can still bowl two games on the dollar fifty a week they give me. I used to be able to, but bowling has gone up, like everything else. A game costs seventy-five cents now, and you still have to rent shoes." Adds his friend: "When I tell my parents I want to buy some records and don't have enough money, they tell me to listen to the radio. They don't understand that I can't hear them enough that way, or when I want to, not some disc jockey."

On the other hand, too much money is not the solution. "One of the boys in my fourth grade class," says a teacher, "gets several dollars a week. He doesn't have many friends and tries to gain some status in the group by displaying his money. Or he'll buy a big bag of candy and dump it on the playground." What this child needs is self-confidence, which his parents can help him to achieve by nurturing some skill or talent; then he won't feel the need to buy friendship.

Too much money only makes children uneasy. "Elementary school children have a certain limited range of values," a suburban Michigan school psychologist claims. "They may talk about what they'll do if they got a lot of money, but they don't actually know how to handle it. It creates problems for them." And teen-agers can run into more problems if too much money comes their way too easily. "I keep allowances small," one father says, "in the hope that drug pushers won't bother kids with no spare cash."

But some parents recognize the necessity of preparing children financially for leaving the nest. "Too many college kids have no idea how to apportion their funds," a banker notes. "They run out of money, borrow, run up bills, get into all sorts of trouble." To forestall such financial inadequacy high school students should go into training, first with a monthly, then a quarterly allowance, including as many predictable expenses as possible: clothing, hobbies, entertainment, car maintenance. "When my fifteen-year-old went away to school," a public relations executive reports, "we put her on a yearly clothing allowance. We negotiated the amount, then she had to budget it for the entire year. I think this lump sum was important. It was a miniature role playing of the business world."

If this approach is to work, parents must stand back, willing to let children either survive or suffer. "Most parents check up too soon," one father says. "They look over the kid's shoulder and get angry at the way he's handling the money. Then they go back to a weekly allowance, without giving him a fair chance."

Whether the allowance is weekly, monthly or quarterly, whatever the age of the child, decide the amount in consultation. He has a big stake in the decision, and he's more likely to be satisfied if he has a voice in the decision-making. "The ground rules should be laid, and the expectations of both parent and child gotten out into the open," says Dr. Norman

Handelman, a child psychologist. "The context, rather than the money itself, is what's important—and open discussion between parent and child sets the right context." But don't think once is enough. Review the decisions regularly, perhaps every couple of months at the beginning, then at least annually. Needs change; so do expectations.

One area of parental expectations often involves a quid pro quo: perform regular chores and you get your allowance, don't hit the baby and you'll get your allowance, earn good grades and you get your allowance.

Children should be expected to contribute to the work of the household, as functioning members of the family unit. Most parents agree. More than 90 percent of the junior and senior high school students surveyed by *Scholastic Magazine's* National Institute of Student Opinion in February 1973 are expected to perform some household chores; only 25 percent are paid for them. It may be a natural inclination to pay kids for the work they do—it teaches them, many parents feel, the value of work and provides motivation for getting the job done—but, say most authorities, it's a mistake to link weekly pocket money with regular family obligations.

A child who is old enough to manage money is old enough to manage some responsibilities at home, if it's just putting his shoes on a shoe rack each evening. Make a milestone out of the child's receiving an allowance, and of his being big enough to help out. But don't make one depend on the other. Excessive expectation of material reward is fostered by paying a child for his every contribution to the family welfare; the result may be a child who won't lift a finger without pay. As Dr. Lee Salk succinctly sums it up: "The parent who pays a child for taking out the garbage is creating a monster."

Some parents find it extremely difficult to give an allowance free and clear, feeling strongly that people don't get something for nothing; children shouldn't get paid if they don't work. "Mary has to set and clear the table; if I have to remind her, she just doesn't get her allowance." A New England school psychologist suggests that this philosophy is closely linked to the

Puritan work ethic that still pervades middle-class values; parents who adhere to this ethic view an allowance given independently of any return as permissive, likely to spoil the child. It helps to remember that the allowance is a learning tool, a device with which children learn to manage money. As such it is as essential to child development as books and toys.

Tying the allowance to behavior or chores may, in any case, backfire. One youngster confided: "I get my allowance on Saturday; if I start to shape up on Thursday, if I volunteer to set the table, my mother forgets how many times she had to remind me to clean my room." Another: "I just don't tell my mother if I goof up on a test; she'll only take away my allowance." These children, it seems, are learning the value of proper appearance, not necessarily of proper behavior; duplicity, although surely unintended, is encouraged. In other words, making the allowance contingent upon performance seldom works; it only casts shadows across the parent-child relationship.

Parents who view the allowance as a learning tool, as the child's share of the family income, do not demand work, or angelic behavior, in return. "An allowance for the kids is like my household money," one mother said. "It depends on what I need, not on the specific chores I do. I yell and scream when they misbehave but I don't touch their allowance." Tying money to behavior conveys the impression, as we have seen, that the child can buy your approval. An angry parent docking an allowance in punishment—although, heaven knows, it's not easy to hand over money to a child who's just been exceedingly rude—is, in effect, denying love, thereby getting love and money all mixed up in the child's mind. Far better to bear firmly in mind that the allowance is an educational device; as such it should no more be taken away than should the privilege of going to school.

Children should be expected to do chores within their capabilities, to do the best they can in school, to behave. When, like all normal children, they fall short, parents should attempt to "make the punishment fit the crime." One woman thinks her mother had the right idea: "I got twenty-six cents a week when I was about ten or eleven, three cents to go downtown and three cents to come back, ten cents for a picture show on Saturday and ten cents for whatever I wanted. If I failed to practice the piano during the week, I couldn't go to the movie because I had to stay home and make up the practice hours—but I got my allowance anyway." Taking away the allowance is rarely an appropriate discipline. Instead it confuses money with the issue at hand, thereby adding to the emotional weight money already bears.

Should you ever supply supplemental funds? A lot of parents do. If, however, you regularly find yourself dispensing predictable amounts above and beyond the allowance, maybe it's time to include those items in the allowance. If Andy is asking to go bowling every week or so, and you supply the money, why not budget it in? That allows him some discretion and you some relief from constant requests.

Then there are the special needs: a class trip, a birthday present, new sheet music. Many families supply extra funds rather than give the child large amounts all year round to meet sporadic needs; others spread the anticipated need across the board; some opt for a combination. "We give Karen a substantial allowance," her mother says, "and expect her to be able to save up for the gifts she wants to buy. We will supply supplemental money for school trips." Rob, on the other hand, gets a small weekly allowance all year—until October 15, when it doubles; he is expected to put aside the extra funds toward Christmas gifts. And Lauren, at ten, gets fifty cents a week. "That's adequate for most of the things she wants," her mother says. "Then, if she wants to buy something more expensive, like the materials to hook a pillow, we'll supply half the cost if she's saved up the other half."

One family dreamed up what they call a contingency fund. "After all, we have unexpected expenses that can't really be budgeted for; every family does. If an appliance needs repair or we want to take a trip, we have funds we can dip into; we think the children should have such a fund as well. So they know we've set aside twenty-five dollars apiece. If a bike needs fixing or the junior high school ski club plans a trip, they can draw on the fund." Other families might take care of the bicycle repair but draw the line at the ski trip; in this family each child knows he has backup funds for the school year, not to be frittered away on ice cream sodas but available for major expenses.

Should children be allowed to borrow ahead? Parents have strong feelings, ranging from, "Of course, we do it all the time when we buy on credit," to, "No, it's a bad habit. They have to learn to manage with what they have." As always, the right answer seems to be flexibility. In general, it's not a good idea for young children to be often in debt. For one thing, their concept of time is not well-developed; a debt that must be repaid over more than a couple of weeks is too long. If the allowance always seems to be inadequate, if the child is always requesting advances, it's time for a review. If you decide his requests are justified, raise the allowance. If you think he's unreasonable, deny the requests for advances. Unless, of course, there's a particular reason, a good one. "Kevin had been saving for months to buy a better guitar than the one he had. When his teacher offered him a very good price on an excellent instrument, he didn't have quite enough money. We thought it would be very foolish for him to miss out, and we advanced him the money. He'll pay it back."

But what if Kevin hadn't wanted to buy a guitar but a set of Parisian postcards? You might not advance him money for a purpose you don't approve, but should you control or supervise the spending of his regular allowance? It's reasonable, say psychologists, to prevent a nine-year-old from buying a dangerous weapon. It's also reasonable to forbid pornography. But this has nothing whatsoever to do with the allowance. It is, instead, a question of "what we do in our house." Money has nothing to do with the limits you set, family values do. Within your family's standards, don't interfere with your child's spending.

This does not imply, however, complete permissiveness. "Children need some controls," a child psychologist notes.

"Without controls they feel uncared for. If parents always say 'decide for yourself,' it can be democratic, or it can be a brush-off. It depends on the context in which it is said. Is it 'do what you want; suffer from your own mistakes' or 'make your own decisions and we'll discuss them with you, sharing your joys and failures?' " The trick, a neat one, is drawing the line between overintrusiveness and not caring at all. But keep the reins loose. Just as an allowance allocated in advance for adult-determined purposes doesn't teach how to handle money, so an allowance too closely supervised doesn't give a child the opportunity to profit by his mistakes. Share your experience with your children, by all means. Tell them if a toy isn't well-made. But if they decide to buy it anyway, it's their decision and money. If they don't ask you in advance, don't even tell them, unless the item involves an outrageous expense.

That's the virtue of starting with small amounts. A child can't make horrendous mistakes if he doesn't have large sums to deal with. When the wheels fall from the plastic car the day after it's purchased, that's the time for you to point out, without reproach, that these cars aren't made very well. By the time he gets older, and has more significant sums to spend, he'll have learned—you hope—to make fewer mistakes.

But remember that emotional satisfaction is derived from the way money is used; children's purchases, just as much as those of adults, fulfill some personal need. Children have to have leeway to buy the things that are important to them, whether it's a rock record you can't tolerate or extra hair ornaments that are just plain superfluous. Think of all the shoes some adults collect, or garden tools, or briar pipes gathering dust on the shelf. Youngsters learn by their mistakes too; either the purchase really does satisfy them, in which case it's not a mistake, no matter what you think, or they won't repeat it. "Anne spent twenty dollars of her carefully saved allowance to get her hair done before she left for camp; at fourteen it was very important for her to make a good impression on the boys. Of course, by the time she got to the waterfront the first day, the set was out. We got a plaintive postcard about how much money she'd wasted."

But Anne wouldn't have learned anything if her parents had prevented the expenditure; she would only have resented their interference. And remembered it. Dr. Benjamin Spock remembers, "I had a mother who was very arbitrary. She was morally right about everything, including what I did with my money. I feel very strongly that a child should be allowed to make his own mistakes with his own money. He won't learn if you try to dictate."

Set reasonable limits, based on your family's values, then don't crowd the child. "My mother doesn't trust me," a junior high school student complains. "What does she think I'm doing? Buying heroin over-the-counter?" Parents have to let go, to allow their children the chance to develop some independence. They will anyway, in the adolescent years, away from home more and more so that you can't really know what they're doing every minute, assuming that you want to. "They reach an age when you can't tell them how to spend their money," the mother of a fifteen-year-old laments. "We have to trust them now." If the groundwork has been correctly laid, there's little cause to worry.

6:

When Children Work

Amy delivers papers. Ted baby-sits. Job stereotypes by sex may be changing, but some verities seem eternal: like millions of red-blooded all-American kids, their forebears and their contemporaries, Amy and Ted like the feeling of earned money jingling in their jeans. It conveys a sense of independence, of power.

Their parents think it's good for them too—but not necessarily for identical reasons. The Puritan ethic that still dominates American middle-class thinking, even in ethnic groups far removed from Pilgrim background, tells us that work is morally good, that it strengthens the character. In families with no need for the money, among children who have every luxury, working nevertheless has status.

Until relatively recently, status was the last reason for Johnny finding a job. Throughout most of the long span of human history, children's physical labor was actually essential to the family, as necessary as the work of their elders. People had children not only because they didn't know how not to but because children had measurable value. Each extra pair of hands was a pair of hands to be put to work, as early as possible, in farmyard and homestead. Whether tending goats, chopping firewood, or making soap, the physical tasks necessary for the family unit's survival were tasks that could be shared, and therefore eased in some measure, by children.

As the country became urbanized and the physical contribution of youngsters diminished, their economic contribution grew. Children went out and earned money, at elementary-school age, because now the money itself was essential for survival. Whether it was working in a mill, shining shoes, or delivering messages, whether the youngsters also managed to attend school or not, each dollar earned was for the good of the family as a whole. Children were needed.

This is no longer true. In the affluence of the 1970s, for the most part, children's earnings are not pre-empted by family need; for the first time they belong to children to spend. "I worked in a grocery store every day after school and all day on Saturday," a Depression-raised businessman recalls, "and it wasn't so I could have money for a car. It was so my family could eat. Now I see my grandson delivering papers and pocketing every cent he makes."

Few people, even with memories like this, resent the affluence that makes it possible for young people to enjoy their earnings. But the result has been a dramatic shift in the way we view our children. They are consumers now, not producers. They are extra mouths to feed, and extra bodies to be put through college, not an extra pair of hands to help.

People don't have children now for the sake of any potential economic contribution; instead the American middle class duplicates itself for more ephemeral, unmeasurable rewards of parenthood. This is all to the good; no one would argue for a return to needing children's work for family survival. At the same time, it isn't good not to be needed. Some observers feel a lack of purpose accounts for many of today's intergenerational problems, for the seeming aimlessness of many adolescents. But most kids can be turned on by the prospect of doing something worthwhile. A real job, with real recognition, still produces real satisfaction. Kids haven't changed that much.

And most parents still think it's a good idea for youngsters to earn some money on their own. Not only does it offset some of the drain on the family exchequer but it gives kids a sense of purpose plus an idea of the relationship between the time and effort necessary to earn a dollar and what that dollar can buy. "My kids are teen-agers," a father complains, "and they still think money grows on trees. They have absolutely no conception of what it takes to earn a buck."

In an era when the value of work by youngsters is based on some vague character-building merit to work itself, on the good it does the worker, rather than on anyone's need, the first work that most kids do consists of household chores. They take the garbage out, set and clear the table, do the dishes, and are more or less responsible for keeping their own rooms neat. As draftees, not volunteers, youngsters do these things because their parents insist. The jobs need doing, and children, just because they're part of the family, should share in the jobs that need doing; parents are absolutely right to expect such co-operation. But let's not glorify these chores and say that they have intrinsic value as work experience, let's not say that children learn anything from them about the real world of work. As one scholarly observer has noted, and innumerable parents can substantiate: "Whether they are done well or poorly, willingly or grudgingly, becomes as much a matter of the parents' skill or the amount of irritation they can induce in the child as of the youngster's pride or responsibility."

Some parents, strongly linked to cause-and-effect morality, try to motivate their children to do these tasks by paying them. Some, throwing up their hands in disgust, don't claim philosophical grounds. "It's the only thing that works," a mother of three insists. "If I don't pay them, they don't do their chores." But, as so often happens, money isn't enough. The children skip the chores anyway, if they can, fight about whose turn it is to do what, and have to be prodded, pushed, and nagged.

One of the problems is that we seldom give children interesting assignments. "I'll never forget moving to the city from a ranch," said a sprightly seventy-year-old lady. "My eleven-year-old son had managed a herd of sheep on the ranch. After we moved to the city he was climbing the walls for lack of activity. I asked around among the neighbors, what they gave their boys to do. 'They empty wastebaskets,' I was told. 'They empty wastebaskets.' It's the only answer I ever got."

Most of us are still geared to this 'empty wastebasket' way of thinking, giving children only the mindless, nasty tasks we prefer not to do ourselves. In part this stems from the complicated gadgetry of life; why ask a child to do what an appliance can do better? But in part, a noted psychologist suggests, there is something unconsciously punitive about giving children only the chores we don't want to do. Are we getting back at them for having life too easy?

There are household chores that have more value as work experience, that offer a challenge and stimulate pride, even when there's no question of monetary reward. Why not give children a crack at these jobs for a change? "My son loves to iron," a mother discovers. "My daughter gets a kick out of switching jobs," another observes. "She thinks it's fun to throw me out of the kitchen and prepare dinner herself once in a while; then I clean up, instead of always leaving the dirty pots for her."

Teach a child to cook or sew, to paint a room or replace a faucet washer, to make a bookshelf or propagate seedlings. "The wrought-iron railing on our front steps was flaking away," says a suburban father, "and had to be sanded, then painted. My nine-year-old daughter volunteered. I wasn't sure she could handle it, but she took enormous care and pride in her work and did a superb job. She was as pleased as punch when she was done—and so was I."

Children like variety, just as adults do, and will often take more interest in a job when it isn't the 'same old thing.' Studies by a Penn State researcher confirm what would seem to be a self-evident truth: The more demanding the task, the more readily it is performed, "in contrast to trivial chores which make little demand on ability or interest." The sense of accomplishment from this kind of assignment, interspersed with the tedious tasks which must still be done, provide some feeling of a real work experience.

Sometimes children ask for pay. "When Janice wanted to be paid for doing the dishes, I asked her how much she thought dinner was worth. She laughed and forgot it. But I realized she needed the chance to earn some money and offered to pay her for cleaning out the basement." Some parents, like Janice's, will pay for "extra" jobs around the house, for the kind of work an outsider might otherwise be hired to do. In one family it might be putting up storm windows each autumn, in another mowing the lawn each week. "I contract with Davey every winter. He gets six dollars for the season to keep our walks clear, no matter how often or how seldom it snows." Other parents, of course, disagree, feeling that outside economic standards should not be applied to the family; any job a child is capable of is one he can do, without pay. "Chris has to shovel our walks, without any pay, because he lives here. And he has to do ours first, before he goes off to earn money from the neighbors."

One family relied on an older child to baby-sit for younger ones. When the teen-ager started getting outside sitting jobs, a compromise was reached. "We pay Gail to sit if she has to give up a paying job to help us out. Otherwise, she sits for nothing." Other parents simply view the family obligation as coming first and don't allow youngsters to take an outside assignment unless they are not needed at home.

And some parents find the whole question defeats them. "I offered to pay for regular lawn raking but wound up having to remind the kids so often that I rescinded the offer and made them rake anyway." Obviously money is not sufficient motivation. As one eighth grader puts it: "I get paid four dollars for mowing the lawn, but I'd rather not be bothered. I'd rather play."

If you choose to pay your children for mowing the lawn,

cleaning out the garage, painting the front porch, or taking down the screens—and you certainly don't have to—keep it as businesslike as possible. Once you bring wages into the picture, you're no longer asking for family help, you're offering a job. Outline the task, offer a realistic rate of pay, and permit your child to refuse the job altogether, just as if he were an outside contractor. If you're going to insist that he do the job anyway, don't imply that you're making a business offer. Then you're only using money as a weapon—and adding to the psychological weight it already bears.

And don't create phony make-work projects to give kids the chance to earn. It's better, says a father who happens to be a banker, to give them the money for what they want than to make up a job. They see right through such strategy, and it's self-defeating.

The surest road to independence, to an understanding of real work and real earnings, now as always, is through work outside the home. There are just too many emotional ramifications clouding the issue when a parent pays and a child receives, even if for real work performed. They can't, after all, give each other up, no matter how poorly a job is performed or how unreasonable the boss. It's little wonder that one study done on the ways in which work enhances maturity among adolescents cites not only the significance of real responsibility, but the sense of accountability derived from working for pay outside the home. Most kids sense this; clearly they prefer doing chores for a neighbor, rather than for their own families—even if both chores and pay are identical.

But a child's first responsibility, his most important work, is school. No job can be allowed to interfere with the time needed to do adequate schoolwork. No job should be allowed to interfere with family obligations, or with a child's health. When a youngster is doing well in school, has ample time for recreation, can fit in his household chores, and still has time to work, the only appropriate response to his eagerness to get out there and earn is "go ahead."

This eagerness is likely to be sparked by parental refusal to foot the bill for some particular heart's desire. "We told Andy if he really wanted that three-hundred-dollar guitar, he had to earn at least half of it. He did—by giving guitar lessons on his old instrument." Sometimes parents deliberately keep a teenager's allowance small, stimulating him to supplement it himself. "When Jim turned sixteen and his social life suddenly expanded, he kept needing money. We put him on a flat ten dollars a month allowance, feeling strongly that he would never become independent if we kept him on handouts. Some of his friends still seem to think money drops from heaven at the wave of a magic wand, or a whine to parents, but Jim knows better. He tutors in math, gives beginner flute lessons, and easily earns twenty dollars a week. And he takes awfully good care of his things now that he expends blood, sweat, and tears to earn them."

He will also be better prepared to leave home, whether for college or full-time employment. For all too many youngsters, the first time they take any financial responsibility upon themselves is after they're away from home. It can be a little late to learn, once sinking is the sole alternative to swimming. Gradual introduction, while still insulated from the consequences of major disaster, is a much better idea.

Most young people like the independence derived from earned income, in the high school years if not before. But what if a youngster isn't interested in finding a job? Parents can suggest, they can urge, but forcing, as in so many other things, frequently backfires. "I thought it would be good for Alan to work, even talked a friend into giving him a job in the store. I was wrong. Alan didn't want to work," his father complains. "He was lazy and careless and, despite friendship, was fired. It was anything but a positive experience." Some children just aren't motivated. Others are simply too swamped by all the other pressures of middle-class life: do well in school (which means hours of homework), join the ball team (and practice every day).

For kids who do want to work, are there still jobs available in this mechanized, prepackaged world? Of course, although it may take a little ingenuity to find them. Teens still caddy, deliver papers, and baby-sit, but they do a lot of other things as well. "Carey got bored with just baby-sitting. Now she and a friend run an afternoon playgroup for three- to five-year-olds twice a week. They take six children and really plan activities for them," Carey's mother reports. "The little ones' mothers are delighted. And Carey and Jill are learning a lot, as well as earning a steady income." Where is this playgroup? In a Manhattan park, refuting the pessimists who claim there are no jobs for youngsters in a big city.

Most jobs can be performed by either boys or girls. Even the courts now recognize that girls can deliver newspapers. But it is true that urban youngsters are limited in certain ways. In areas dominated by apartment houses there are no garden chores or snow-removal assignments for kids. There often aren't even paper routes. But there are other jobs. Where grocery shopping is not done by car but on foot, for example, children can carry bags home from the market for individual shoppers—or deliver for the store itself.

Timothy is a city boy. Asked to care for house plants by a traveling neighbor, he expanded operations and now waters plants and tends birds and fish throughout his apartment complex. Andrea walks dogs, a popular service in both city and suburb, and one open to youngsters of almost any age. Sheila did so well in her eighth-grade typing class that she gets fifty cents a page for helping an overburdened church office with its typing chores. Jonathan gives magic shows at children's parties; he started at eleven and now, at sixteen, has parlayed a hobby into substantial income.

In all of these jobs youngsters learn to fulfill a commitment. Whether it's walking dogs twice a day every day, or doing two magic shows a month, a job accepted must be a job performed. Accountability is inherent in the assignment. Newspapers on the roof, and the paper boy loses his route. Howling dogs, overanxious to go out and disturbing the neighbors, and the dog-walker loses her job. Disappointed partygoers, and the magician loses referrals.

These positive learning elements are generally not present within the family, since family members do, and really should, help one another out. If the dog has to be walked and the dog-walker is busy with an after-school soccer match, mother often does the walking. If the lawn is to be mowed and a swimming party is formed, the mowing waits a day. Paid jobs, for outside employers, don't allow this leeway.

Good volunteer jobs offer some of the same benefits—and they're sometimes easier to secure than paid employment, especially for younger teens. A summer spent working in a day-camp program, an after-school tutoring commitment, volunteer work at a local hospital—all can help a youngster develop both skills and reliability. In either volunteer or paid employment, however, parents must be careful to stand back. Let the child take the responsibility. The mother who drives the paper boy along his route every time it rains is doing him a disservice. Overprotection is the worst enemy of maturity.

Wage-earners, of course, learn a bit more about managing money as such. Sometimes they accept a going rate of pay, sometimes they set their own fee; either way they have to collect the money and keep track of it. If paid by check, they learn something about banking, in the most immediate way possible. They also learn about human nature. One fourteen-year-old says: "I don't like working by the hour. People say I'm never fast enough. I try to set a flat fee." His friend adds: "People pay more, usually, than what I would ask, so I try not to set a price at all."

The interest in working seems to be stronger than ever. Of 11,870,000 fourteen- to nineteen-year-old boys in this country on March 1, 1972, the Department of Commerce reports, 58 percent earned income, as did 48 percent of the 11,791,000 girls. The Rand Youth Poll reports that, at the end of 1972, youngsters' earnings were at an all-time high. Even eight- and nine-year-olds added average earnings of seventy-five cents a week to their allowances. Ten- to twelve-year-olds averaged a dollar and a quarter in earnings, thirteen- to fifteen-year-olds earned three dollars and sixty cents, and sixteen- to nineteen-year-olds raked in over twelve dollars a week. This earned income, plus allowances, adds up to formidable spending power: eight- to twelve-year-olds spent $2.2 billion in 1972; their thirteen- to nineteen-year-old brothers and sisters spent $24 billion. No wonder advertisers court the youth market.

Do advertisers have free rein? Or do parents influence the way young people spend their hard-earned money?

Of course, parents have influence. Without saying a word, all the values instilled in the preceding years have an impact when it comes to spending the money youngsters earn. But one of the toughest questions for parents is the question of direct control over youngsters' earnings. If we subscribe to the theory that allowance money may be freely spent, within the bounds of family standards, and that this freedom is what teaches the uses and limits of money, what about earned money? Perhaps the principle should be the same—but the amounts involved may be so much greater that many parents hesitate to permit such freedom.

"I use whatever I earn to go bowling, and try to get in three or four games a week," says a suburban ninth grader, whose mother wonders, occasionally, whether some of that money shouldn't be banked. Other youngsters collect coins, or stamps, or airplane models, and expend large sums in the pursuit of these hobbies. Some buy comic books, others go skiing. Should parents set limits? Can they?

As always, it depends on the family structure. In authoritarian families, what the parents say goes, about money as about everything else. "I don't let him carry any money around with him," says the father of an eleven-year-old, "and I don't let him accumulate too much in his wallet at home. When it gets up to fifteen dollars or so, I take it and put it in the bank. Sometimes I let him keep some change." "Jill can keep enough of her baby-sitting money for a movie every other week," the mother of this sixteen-year-old says. "The rest goes in the bank, period." "I don't care where the money comes from, whether I earned it or he did," says the father of a twenty-year-old college student. "There'll be no spending on foolishness."

Sometimes parental attitudes depend on the amount at stake. "Steve delivers a weekly shopping guide in the neighborhood, at two cents a paper," his father reports. "It doesn't add up to very much, so I don't say much about it. But he was really shocked one day when I told him that when he gets older, and earns more, he'll have to contribute toward room and board. I guess he assumes it's our obligation to support him forever."

In more and more families, the child's earnings are his to spend without question. If there's really no need for the child to pay his own way, many parents feel uncomfortable about asking for his contribution. "It can't be more than a token payment, anyway," one midwestern parent says. "He might as well enjoy the fruits of his labors."

But does enjoying it mean spending it all on trivia? Or can he be expected to, at least, cover some of the optional expenses for which his parents usually fork out extra money? You wouldn't ask a fourteen- or fifteen-year-old to pay for all his clothing, or the food—even if excessive—he consumes at the family dinner table. But a free public high school can cost a good deal by the time graduation rolls around, in so-called optional extras: yearbooks, field trips, sporting events. Should earning children cover some of these expenses for themselves? It's not a bad idea, but each individual family will decide for itself. Sometimes it's the parent who decides what's important—and therefore pays for it. "I never could afford my high school ring," says one mother. "Now I want my daughter to have hers and she's not really interested. I'm going to buy it because I think she'll be glad someday."

Where the item is important to the youngster, however, there's usually little discussion. He simply takes over, delighted to be able to pay his own way. "I feel like a baby," says a fifteen-year-old, "if I have to ask my mother for money to go to the school football game." It's a necessary part of growing up to be able to decide what to do and to do it, without consultation on each individual occasion.

This independence is a natural by-product of the part-time

job. But some children cannot find jobs, or need all their time for study, and earning money should not be a prerequisite for participating in school events. Such extracurricular activities are as much a part of education as the classroom experience.

While independence is a desirable goal, parents retain an obligation to supervise the doings of children, an obligation not diminished because the child earns money. At the least, a banker suggests, there should be an auditing process, a monthly accounting of earnings and expenditures. "If the parents act as independent financial advisors, a review of outgo can be a constructive exercise." The clue, of course, is objectivity, an ability on the part of parents to analyze their own youngster's money management dispassionately. This may be too much to ask, given the emotional involvement of parents and children, so perhaps the best route to take is negotiation in advance.

Purpose is the significant factor, suggests Bernard S. Yudowitz, a Massachusetts psychiatrist who works with adolescents: Why did he get a job in the first place? If he sought work because he wants to buy a trumpet, or a ten-speed bicycle, and his parents agreed, then his earnings can go to this end. If he's working because his parents urged him to earn some money toward the high cost of college, then the money, or the bulk of it, gets saved for college. "There's no question about it. If Lynn wants to go to college, her baby-sitting money goes in the bank. She does want to go, plans to be a speech therapist, and constantly seeks baby-sitting jobs."

But another parent says: "Alice earned a thousand dollars one summer. We didn't insist on it being earmarked for college because we didn't want her to choose a college on the basis of paying for it." That's something to think about, too.

If there was no particular goal, then what? "Jeanne earns fifteen to twenty dollars most weeks as a bread-and-butter girl in a local restaurant. She thought for a while she wanted to travel and was saving it. Now she's decided just to spend what she earns. I think she has more blouses than any other sixteen-year-old in three counties." Jeanne's mother thinks so many blouses are silly; should she prevent Jeanne from buying them? No, not unless the family needs the money. Ultimately, Jeanne herself may realize that there are more significant things she can do with her money. Or, if blouses continue to give her satisfaction, she'll continue to buy them.

As a tool, we have to keep reminding ourselves, money is used to buy the things we need and want. We derive emotional rewards, a sense of inner satisfaction, in many ways, including through purchasing things that please us. In Jeanne's case, it's blouses, at least for now. For another, it might be coins, or books, or shoes, or as much bowling as possible. It doesn't really matter. As long as the fascination isn't destructive, it's important that a youngster be allowed to fulfill his needs—and important that he can do it through earned income, his own money and not his parents.

But he must define his needs. "He can't spend it all on bowling and come to me for money to buy a football ticket," a parent insists. "I think he has to learn to set priorities, to decide which is more important. Otherwise, he's back to leaning on handouts and thinking the pocket is bottomless."

At the same time, Dr. Yudowitz insists, a child should not be permitted to undercut the family's value system through his own earnings. It's reasonable to require that a youngster buy his own gasoline when he uses the family automobile, but buying gasoline does not imply automatic permission to use the car. He needn't be permitted to assume, without discussion, that his earnings are his to spend right away. Through negotiation, the purposes of his income should be clearly stated. Then, if a parent finds money being spent unwisely—for too many late evenings at the local hangout, for example—he has the right to step in and assume control. This, as with allowances, is more a matter of what the parents consider acceptable behavior than it is a money matter; money is just what makes the behavior possible.

Of course, if earnings are too rigidly restricted, so that the youngster derives no satisfaction from his work, he may decide it's not worth working. It's better, if possible, to strike a balance.

We've been talking here about youngsters up to the age of seventeen or so, youngsters pursuing part-time jobs while in school. They really should be permitted to enjoy the fruits of their labors, while gradually assuming some of the expenses associated with school and recreation.

With older workers, those working full-time while living at home, it's a different story. Parents can reasonably expect such wage-earners to cover their own expenses, and to contribute toward room and board. When they don't, in fact, they may be building up troubles for the day when they establish their own families. Sociologists point to fragmentation of family life created by each worker regarding his earnings as strictly his own, an outlook generated, at least in part, by the way in which parents regard children's earnings. "He'll only be young once. Let him spend his earnings on fun. We can afford to take care of him," is, for a twenty-three-year-old, an indulgence that confers no favors. Men who control the family's income, while doling out a household allowance, and women who assume that if they work their earnings are theirs alone, to spend on luxuries—both stem from a milieu of "what's mine is all mine." Both were led to believe that selfishness is natural. At some point the common good, the interests of the family, must take precedence—and the groundwork for this is laid when a child first begins to work.

7:

The Shopping Syndrome

Kids, most kids, are inveterate shoppers. From the first penny clutched in a pudgy fist to a long summer's wages, money seems to burn a hole in the proverbial pocket. From toddler days onward, children relish the delights of the marketplace.

As we saw earlier, emotional needs are frequently met through shopping: a need for independence, for self-gratification, for peer approval, for security. But what about the purely practical? When and how do children learn to shop? What do they spend their money on? And how can we, as parents, teach them to shop wisely?

The lessons start before we know it. "Each child in the middle class is automatically a consumer trainee before he can walk," sociologist David Riesman wrote in *The Lonely Crowd*, "and his practice in consumer research begins long before he can count change." Every time a child sees money change hands, every time he hears parents compare value, set priorities, make a purchasing decision, every time he himself has coins to spend, every time his friends praise a product ("This new game is neat!"), and, not least, every time television tells him to buy, he is learning how to be a consumer.

Before toddlers comprehend the functional value of money, long before they understand *why* it can be exchanged for so many lovely things, they think this special something must have magical qualities. Three-year-old Allison doesn't understand anything about money as a medium of exchange—but she knows quite clearly that something called a quarter can be swapped for chocolate-coated ice cream on a stick. Because she loves to imitate Mommy, just as all three-year-olds do, and Mommy does a lot of shopping, Allison eagerly plays "store" —just as eagerly as she plays "house" or "doctor." And she is aided in her efforts by that fundamental prop, the toy cash register.

Despite Allison's fascination she remains, of course, unsophisticated. Offered coins, she will invariably take two pennies over one quarter; quantity is what counts at this age. But she relishes handling money, real money. "If she's with me in a store," Allison's mother reports, "she insists on handing over the money to the cashier. It can take forever if I let her. So I usually try to give her just one thing to pay for, with the exact change." Despite understandable maternal impatience, Allison is busy learning. She is learning the principle of exchange, the principle she won't fully understand, according to Anselm Strauss' studies, until she's about five. But the lesson isn't lost; the accumulated impressions build up, combining with other impressions of the marketplace, layer upon layer, until a consumer—spendthrift, penny-pincher or happy medium—is formed.

Three- and four-year-olds, an experienced nursery school director comments, do understand that purchasing involves some sort of exchange, but they're rather vague about the details. "When the children play store they never ask for something without offering something in return—either another toy, as a barter, or what they'll call money, a piece of paper or a block. But it has nothing to do with equivalent value—it's just the idea of an exchange."

As Allison and her friends grow older, as they're exposed to more shopping with the family, they begin to realize that barter doesn't count; it's money that plays the crucial role. But even then, even after youngsters can name all the coins, and realize that a nickel will buy more candy than a penny, and a dime more than either, most still see purchases as an even exchange: so many pennies for so much candy. "No," says Kevin firmly, "I can't buy penny candy if you give me a nickel; I have to buy nickel candy." This impression persists for some time; mothers who dispatch first graders on errands generally find it wiser, if at all possible, to provide the exact change.

Parents can take advantage of the normal lively curiosity of preschoolers. Chances are you can't escape having Junior along when you shop, at least not often, so seize the opportunity to teach him his first lessons in consumerism. Let him select the package you want, physically take it from the shelf. Let him pay for some items. Most important, take the time to explain why you choose one product over another. Kids like reasons. The same youngster who insists on a particular brand of sneakers, "because they'll make me run faster," will accept, "this cereal is better for us than that one, that's why I buy it."

Try to explain your negative responses too. He may be driving you batty with the gimmie's—after all, stores spread their wares so enticingly—but, says a marketing executive, "vague, unsatisfactory answers given just to put a child off don't teach him anything, don't satisfy him, and don't stop the requests." If you don't want him to have candy because it's bad for his teeth, or because it's too close to dinner time, say so. He'll understand—even if he doesn't agree. Some mothers find a solution in offering the youngster a choice: "You may pick out one treat on this trip, a box of raisins or peanut butter crackers, and that's all." Some make it a preliminary form of allowance, even for a toddler: "You may have ten cents. After you pick out something in this store that costs ten cents, that's all."

Today's young sophisticates are no strangers to the marketplace. Even before they fully understand it, even before age five, they are bombarded with product information via television, urged to express product preferences to their families. And they do. A recent syndicated cartoon spoofed the hard sell: on the screen an announcer is depicted urging his young viewers to "tell Mommy to buy." As a baby too young to talk wonders, in cartoon fashion, how she can convey the message, the announcer continues " . . . and I want all you babies who can't talk to start crying and point to the TV set!!" Ninety-four percent of all mothers interviewed in a 1956 study by Eugene Gilbert and Company reported that their children asked them to buy things seen on television. Over half of a group of five-year-olds studied by James U. McNeal of the University of Oklahoma suggested brand-name items on family shopping trips, suggestions that were frequently accepted. Not only do parents often accept children's suggestions, in this era sociologists have characterized as both affluent and permissive, they often seriously consult their offspring, soliciting their opinions on what to buy. "Sure I buy the kind of cereal he wants," says a mother of her four-year-old. "Why not? He's the one who's going to eat it."

Five-year-olds, brand-conscious as they are, McNeal found, have little real interest in money as such. Most of the fives in this study receive a small weekly allowance, more from social custom than from need, and take a lot of time spending it, making their decisions at point of purchase. This is the child who takes three-quarters of an hour, driving his mother to distraction, to select a "special" pencil in the dime store. It's a child who rarely, if ever, shops alone. And it's a child, often, who puts his money down and forgets all about it.

At some point between five and seven, however, there seems to be a giant step in comprehension, a suddenly acquired ability to assume the consumer role. By seven, McNeal found, most youngsters realistically see money as a necessity for acquiring goods, and often save for future purchases as well as spending for immediate gratification. "I buy a pack of baseball cards when I get my allowance," says one second grader, "and save part of it. When I get enough, I want to buy a big package of soldiers." Fads are important at this age—baseball cards or stick-ons or whatever the crowd is buying. Seven-year-olds frequently shop alone or with friends. They also, with their broadening knowledge of the world, influence more and more family purchases.

As children grow, as they have more disposable income coupled with increasing independence, they become more and more involved in the marketplace. In these years, the elementary school years, they learn a great many consumer lessons from parents, both through example and through direct teaching. "I showed Douglas how to figure out prices and why one box of cereal was a better buy than another. It really paid off," says this Denver mother. "Doug is eight now and he loves doing the arithmetic when we shop. He picked out a bag of chocolate chips that, per ounce, was more reasonable than another brand." This kind of lesson can be quickly applied to personal experience. "Candy is a lot cheaper if we buy it outside the movies," an eleven-year-old observes.

There are other lessons. On value for the money: "She didn't have to go to Woolworth's to save money," says a New York father. "I pointed out Japanese stores where she could buy a well-designed vase for her grandmother for seventy cents. Children don't always realize the variety of stores there are." Outside New York or other major urban centers, the choice may not be quite as broad, but there are choices. Housewares or hardware stores often have interesting family gift ideas; so do stationery stores. Dime stores, including Woolworth's, can be shopped wisely too, if children are shown how to choose. "I told Andrea a plant makes a great gift, or note paper, or a coffee mug; she doesn't have to get handkerchiefs or perfume."

On bargain-hunting: "Elizabeth used to think my bargain-hunting was peculiar," a Connecticut mother says of her thirteen-year-old. "Now she realizes that shopping around is a good idea, that you might get things on sale that you couldn't have otherwise." Some eager youngsters carry this lesson beyond their parents' desire to economize. One New Jersey teen buys all her blouses at a charity thrift shop. "In a way, I suppose she's being sensible," her mother says. "She gets a lot more blouses this way. But, in another way, I hope nobody sees her in there."

There are still other lessons in food shopping. Kids need experience in shopping—we all learn best by experience—and running errands for the family is at least as valuable a learning tool (in addition to helping the family) as is shopping for bubble gum and baseball cards. Send them on errands where they'll have the chance to exercise discretion, even if some mistakes are unavoidable. "My son was so pleased because he saved so much on an extra-large size of mustard, I didn't have the heart to complain about how much space it will take up forever in the refrigerator," one mother remembers. "But the next time I sent him shopping I tactfully pointed out that the large economy size isn't always the best buy, not if we can't use it up in a reasonable length of time."

Another mother suggests a successful technique: "I used to take the kids to the market with me when I was pressed for time. I would ask them to find a couple of things, bring them to me, and go for the next set. I did most of the marketing, as a result, and they didn't get much out of it. Last time we went I divided the list in three and gave each of the kids (they're ten and thirteen) a written list; we each took a cart and shopped independently. I wouldn't have thought it would make so much difference, but the kids were delighted. They were totally pleased with themselves—and we got done much faster."

By nine or ten, marketing educator James McNeal notes, youngsters have a simple understanding of the marketing process. They can discuss the sources of products, the function of stores, the concept of profit. They are capable of assuming more responsibility for family shopping. And they experiment with the principles of capitalism on their own, exploring it from different angles. "John was regularly augmenting his allowance by selling his outgrown toys to his younger brother. Every time Jimmy got his allowance, John offered him a 'special purchase.' We finally had to put a stop to it." Other children run garage sales, sponsor a backyard carnival, or set up a card table on the sidewalk to sell lemonade or surplus toys. Sometimes it's for a worthy cause, a recognized charity; more often the worthy cause is the youngster himself.

Then there are the seed sellers, closely related to the greeting-card purveyors. Those colorful full-page comic book come-ons entice today's younger set just as they did our generation; some of the ads don't seem to have changed a bit. The glowing promise of prizes, then as now, may too often be tantalizingly beyond reach, but the experience of buying and selling itself, of marketing wares, can be a valuable introduction to basic economics, especially for children ambitious enough to extend their selling efforts beyond Grandma and Aunt Martha.

This is a good time to teach budgeting, the basics of planning ahead. Some children realize instinctively that you can do more with money by waiting till you have more; others need guidance. "We've tried to create a sense of priorities, an appreciation of things money can be used for," says a father who is also a professor of economics, "that if you don't blow it on the bubble-gum machine every day, you can do some extraordinary things with it."

The extraordinary things become more visible to children as they have more money—the earned income of the seed seller or the baby-sitter, the enlarged allowance of the adolescent. Hand in hand with the ability to buy more should go responsibility—responsibility for making their own purchasing decisions and responsibility for caring for the things they purchase.

A province in which both boys and girls can assume more responsibility than they are often allowed is in meeting their own clothing needs. Most parents plan, usually vaguely, to have the children take over—sometime or other. With no specific plan, however, we frequently drift along and wake up, with the child ready for college or well along in high school, to the fact that we've really given no responsibility at all. It's better, as in most things, to start small—with socks and fancy sneaker laces, belts and embroidered jeans patches. Move up to shirts and, eventually, to the jeans themselves.

There are several possible approaches: you can supply the money for each individual purchase, letting the child make the actual selection as the need arises, or you can budget a specified amount, with the child, for a specified period of time, thereby giving him greater latitude. Or, you can provide the basics and have the child, with his own money, purchase accessories. "We don't have nearly so many arguments over things Leslie 'has' to have now that she does the buying," Leslie's mother notes. "I buy her school wardrobe in the fall, shopping with her, including any accessories that are necessary to complete an outfit. Then, if she feels she has to have extra hair ribbons, belts, scarves, jewelry, etc., etc., etc., she has to buy them herself, out of her allowance. We did increase her allowance somewhat, under this arrangement, but it's worth every penny. She's spending less, I think, and we don't fight all the time. And she's actually a lot less careless with her belongings—the scarf she paid for isn't as likely to get left at a friend's house." Financial writer Sylvia Porter confirms this mother's observation: children who buy their own clothes, she says, tend to be more conservative about spending. And one ten-year-old I know, whose mother has been buying birthday presents for the endless parties of her school friends, trying to keep the outlay minimal, remarked, "If I had to buy the presents, I wouldn't spend as much." Says her mother: "As soon as I heard that, I decided to increase her weekly allowance and let her buy the gifts. She'll certainly learn more about what things cost, and how hard it is to buy something nice for a couple of dollars."

A Long Island mother of three girls has gone a step further than most in allocating responsibility. "I kept track of what we spent on clothing for a year, then put each girl on a budget.

The ten-year-old was allowed a hundred and fifty dollars for the year, the fifteen- and sixteen-year-olds two hundred each. I keep the money and keep the accounts, but it has eliminated a lot of hassles. They don't ask for things they don't actually need. In fact, when I wanted them to have dresses for a special occasion, I had to offer to pay—they didn't want to spend their own money."

When you do let children shop for themselves, try to have the fortitude to let them learn from their own mistakes. It isn't always easy. When a young man in Atlanta bought a boutique shirt that shrank to postage stamp size on its first washing, his parents promptly suspended his shopping privileges. Their reaction is understandable. But chances are he wouldn't have repeated the same mistake—and he would have profited from the experience.

It's far better to let children learn while they're young, difficult as it may be, because, as they get older, they play with increasingly larger amounts of cash.

One way of estimating what kids actually have is by looking at what they spend. The grand total in 1973, according to the Rand Youth Poll: thirteen- to nineteen-year-olds spent $24.7 billion, while their eight- to twelve-year-old siblings accounted for $2.5 billion. Not exactly peanuts.

As of December 1972, Rand reports, thirteen- to fifteen-year-old boys had an average income, composed of both allowances and earnings, of $6.85 a week, of which they spent $5.55. Girls of this age had income of $7.10 a week and spent $6.10, putting the rest aside for longer-range purchases. The figures show a steady curve, as young people manage to keep pace with the inflationary spiral: a year earlier the boys' income was $6.00 a week, of which $5.05 was spent; the girls had $6.20 and spent $5.30. While the girls received a bit less in allowance from parents, they managed to earn more, largely through baby-sitting.

How do youngsters spend this money of their own? The first major interest, and a perpetual one, is food. An analysis of children and their money prepared by Dr. Scott Ward of Harvard for *Outside/In,* a banking publication, indicates that 36 percent of kindergarteners spend their money on food as do 29 percent of third graders and 17 percent of sixth graders. The Rand surveys show that an interest in food is persistent among all income groups. The need to share an after-school snack with friends apparently spans economic brackets. Eight- and nine-year-old boys, comparable to the third graders Dr. Ward interviewed, spend seventy cents a week on snacks, out of a total income of $1.50. "Every time I put Ralph's jeans in the wash," his mother says in exasperation, "I find candy wrappers stuffing the pockets." Ten- to twelve-year-olds spent $1.05 on snacks out of $2.65; thirteen- to fifteen-year-olds spent $1.90 out of $5.55, and sixteen- to nineteen-year-olds, where for the first time snacks move out of first place, spent $2.30 on snacks out of $17.85. By these later teen years, the girls either aren't as hungry or are diet-conscious—or are having their snacks paid for by the boys; they spend only $1.35 a week on snacks out of $18.90.

In the early years boys and girls have similar interests: magazines and comics, records, toys and "stuff." As they get a little older, they spend more on hobbies and collections— "Larry's coin collection is the biggest thing in his life this year"—and begin to put away some money toward larger purchases: cameras, bikes, watches, radios. Ten- to twelve-year-olds begin going to the movies, and spend about fifty cents a week in the pursuit of big-screen entertainment, a figure that jumps to $1.45 for thirteen- to fifteen-year-old boys and $1.15 for the girls. Sixteen- to nineteen-year-old boys spend an average of $4.60 a week on movies and entertainment; girls of the same age spend only $2.40. Despite the women's movement, boys still seem to incur the largest share of dating costs.

Clothing and cosmetics take up more and more of the teen-age girl's attention, and her pocketbook, as she gets ready for the dates the teen-age boy is paying for. "Amy is twelve," says her mother, "and at the age where she spends every penny she can at the cosmetics counter. She comes home with the most awful junk—eye makeup of all kinds, mostly." Thirteen-to fifteen-year old-girls, says Rand, spend an average of ninety-five cents a week on cosmetics and fragrances, and another fifty-five cents on "jewelry, trinkets and notions." By the next age bracket, sixteen to nineteen, young women spend $3.60 on smelling sweet and looking pretty, plus $1.80 on "jewelry, trinkets and notions," and another $1.50 a week on beauty parlor and hair products.

Marketers are well aware of this interest and do all they can to promote it. The U.S. Department of Commerce, George Schiele, President of Mailbag International, said to advertisers in August 1973, reports that the average middle-class teen has fifteen dollars to spend weekly. "Multiply that," Schiele said, "by the fifteen million teen girls who hang out at the cosmetics counters of their local drug stores."

For years, *Seventeen* magazine has been taking the pulse of its readership. Its Market Fact Sheet of July 1, 1973, reports that the 14,149,000 young women between thirteen and nineteen constitute 13 percent of all U.S. females and have an estimated annual income from just earnings and allowance of $8.8 billion. This 13 percent of the female population, *Seventeen* reports, account for 20 percent of all women's beauty expenditures and 23 percent of all women's and children's apparel expenditures. In the fall of 1972, in preparation for the school year, high school girls spent an average of $296.48 on clothing, for a total dollar volume, in the high school market alone, of $2,224,818,000.

This volume seems incredible against the jeans-and-sandals fashions of today. Actually, it seems, these styles have had more of an impact on the college level; freshmen entering college in the fall of 1973, according to *Seventeen* research, spent less than their high school sisters on clothing. And the college girl of 1973 spent less than her older sister in the cashmere sweater days of 1956. "It's so disappointing," one mother says. "I was looking forward to outfitting my daughter for college, remembering what fun it was going shopping with my mother. I should have known—all Alice wants is some new jeans and shirts." But, somehow, the money adds up, even if invested in jeans, to an average of $296.48 per high school girl and $275.85 per college freshman.

While they may not care much about clothes, young people feel very free about spending. Brought up in years of virtually unbroken prosperity—the economic downturns we've known since World War II haven't affected middle-class affluence to any significant extent—they see no reason to be anything but optimistic about the future. Because they see nothing but a rosy glow on the horizon, a future that will care for itself, they take money for granted and feel free to spend it on whatever suits them. It's an echo of the toddler's belief in his parents' bottomless pocket and his own being central to the universe. Teen-age girls have no qualms about spending on clothes and cosmetics, or boys on sports and cars; there will always be more cash where that came from.

Teens have a passion for acquisition, Andrew MacLeod, then advertising director of *Seventeen* magazine, wrote in *Media-Scope* in September 1969; they are avid to try anything new. Teen-age girls are spendthrifts, he notes. "They have lived from earliest memory in an affluent society and care little about price for two reasons, one practical and one psychological. Their fathers are at their earning peaks, and have the income to satisfy daughter's whims. In addition, they want what they want when they want it, regardless of cost." Aaron Cohen, currently research director of *Seventeen*, says that far from being casual about money, "a teen-ager is the most wary shopper around. She really looks before she plunks down her money. But," Cohen goes on, "at the same time teens are the number-one tryers, eager to sample any new product. And, if they see something they really want, then the cost factor goes out the window."

This eagerness to buy leads to the impulsive shopping characteristic of the teen years. In *An Analysis of the Teen-Age Market,* Philip R. Cateora of the University of Colorado notes that 65 percent of the approximately two hundred teen-agers he surveyed agree that shopping around for the best price is desirable. But, when asked what they themselves would actually do, fully 60 percent admitted that they would buy at the first store that had what they wanted. Knowing what to do and doing it are two quite different things.

Lester Rand of the Rand Youth Poll confirms these observations. "Kids are big impulse buyers," he says, "with a tendency to squander. They save up two or three dollars, buy something, and find they don't even want it a couple of days later. Thrift doesn't mean anything today and 'a penny saved is a penny earned' is completely out. Instant gratification is all that matters." "Why do you buy so much junk?" a mother asks. "I can't even turn around in your room anymore."

In this atmosphere of easy spending, young people influence one another to an enormous extent. It starts early. McNeal notes that the five- to nine-year-olds he studied all admitted being influenced by their friends and, in turn, influencing their friends when it came to making purchases. Kids want things their friends have. They talk over their purchasing plans. They shop in groups. "I always thought I was safe if my daughter approved her own clothing," one mother ruefully notes. "I gave up bringing things home for her when she was seven. But I discovered it wasn't good enough. She was nine when we bought school shoes that her friends subsequently disapproved. I refused to replace them, of course, but it was a fight every time I insisted that she wear them. She would have worn her sneakers every single day until those shoes were outgrown, in mint condition, if I had let her."

Adolescents, as every parent knows all too well, don't outgrow the need for their friends' approval. If anything, it gets even worse. In the social uncertainty of the teen years, the approval of friends is all-important. Passion for popularity, H. H. Remmers and D. H. Radler wrote in *Scientific American*, translates itself into almost universal conformity. "Don't be ridiculous, Mother, I can't wear a skirt to school if everyone else is wearing jeans."

Do parents, then, have any influence over the way kids spend their money? Yes, of course. As a bare minimum, George Schiele points out, parents have some control over the amounts of money young people have to spend. And, in addition, parental spending habits over the years provide an example. (This works in both directions. Lester Rand claims that adults of the 1970s are just as thoughtless impulse buyers as are young people. "I was going to buy you a pocket calculator for your birthday," the children hear their mother say in annoyance to their father, "couldn't you wait a week?")

Overall family values do have an impact, even when children don't seem to respond to suggestions about individual purchases. But brand choice, says Schiele, is an important way for kids to set their own standards, to assert their independence from their parents. This is a necessary part of growing up. A ten-year-old, he points out, washes her hair with shampoo picked by her mother; a twenty-year-old is an adult, with almost no influence from parents. In the intervening decade there is a gradual transition from dependence to independence. "Kids make a real effort to substitute in every way possible, as quickly as possible, their choice for those of their parents. Brand choices fall naturally into this because they are low-resistance items. Mother may fight about behavior, about staying out all night, but she won't fight about choice of shampoo."

With the well-marked youth orientation of society as a whole, some observers say, the influence flows in the other direction. Products and fashions are designed to suit youth—"try and find a flattering style if you're over thirty-five," a businessman complains—and parents are more likely to consult their offspring than the other way round. Twenty-five years ago, Andrew MacLeod of *Seventeen* wrote, a girl under twenty depended on her mother; today a teen-age girl is not only independent in buying clothes—but her mother often asks *her* fashion advice.

There is, some think, a bit of a trend away from this youthful influence, just in the last year or so. "Young people are no longer dictating fashion," says marketing executive Melvin Helitzer, "and they themselves are showing a bit more individuality, not just running with the pack when it comes to selecting clothes." But some parents aren't so sure. "My ten-year-old daughter—who will wear nothing but pants herself, for both school and play—has very definite ideas about what I should wear," one mother notes. "I don't necessarily agree with her all the time. But if I'm not quite sure, she can make me uncomfortable. I've changed my clothes sometimes at her suggestion, and then wondered what on earth I was doing."

Whether or not youthful styles are still dominating the fashion scene, there's little doubt that young people have a strong impact on family purchases. In addition to the necessary items a family must buy, simply because it contains children, youthful opinions and preferences influence optional purchases. From the four-year-old who picks out the breakfast cereal to the teen-ager who talks Dad into buying a sports car (young people led the trend to smaller cars, says Melvin Helitzer), young people make their wishes known. Whether it's the family toothpaste or the place to go on vacation, the voice of the offspring is heard in the family.

Because their influence is so substantial, because kids themselves have so much money to spend, it becomes all the more important that they learn to spend it wisely. Schools in many parts of the country are coming to the aid of parents and beginning to teach consumer education, not the introduction to economics courses that many of us found so theoretical in high school, so irrelevant in daily life, but practical means of coping with an ever-more-complex marketplace: how to budget, determine value, buy on credit, purchase a house or insurance. Most of the classes are on the high school level, but some innovative tacks are being taken as early as the preschool years.

Although most nursery schools have toy cash registers and some a mock storefront as well, few try specifically to teach consumerism. An exception is the demonstration preschool at Glassboro State College in southern New Jersey, where home economics consultant Lois Winand is developing a consumer education program for three- and four-year-olds. "They can understand a surprising variety of consumer concepts, even at this age," she insists: that things that look good to eat may not be safe, that clothing you care for lasts longer. Using the mock storefront in one object lesson, Mrs. Winand teaches comparative pricing. She divides the class into two groups, giving each $2.50, and asks them to "buy" enough cookies, juice and paper cups for the group. In doing so, the toddlers discover that they have more money left over when they buy one box of one hundred paper cups then if they buy two boxes of fifty cups each. These children can't add yet—but when they play store in free-play time, they talk about package sizes and prices, proving that the lessons sink in, lessons that parents can teach on family shopping expeditions.

In teaching consumer education, schools seem to be, at last, meeting the needs of a society based on consumption. This represents a fundamental shift in the traditional approach to education, according to Thomas Brooks, dean of home economics at Southern Illinois University, Carbondale, and chairman of the consumer education committee of the Consumer Federation of America. "In our educational system," he says, "we've taught what's essential to earn a living but we've never given any thought to helping youngsters make decisions on how to use the money they earn. The stress has been on producing rather than consuming, a one-sided approach which is giving way to a more balanced curriculum."

Setting priorities is the key to intelligent consumerism. Even the Glassboro preschoolers recognize that decisions have to be made. "My mommy wanted a pocketbook but she had to buy me a snowsuit," a four-year-old volunteers. Even small children can learn the difference between needs and wants, between the things a family must buy and the things it chooses to buy when possible. While every parent may not be an expert on the stock market, or on the fine points of insurance—courses taught in some Illinois high schools under that state's legislated consumer education curriculum—every parent can get across this most important consumer concept: making choices.

Children absorb a certain amount of this, just through overhearing parental decision-making, but we can stress the process, bring it to their level, more than we ordinarily might. Just asking a small child, consumer educators suggest, whether he would rather have a vanilla or a chocolate ice cream cone sets the stage, getting across the message that there is a choice to be made and that he can make the choice for himself. He has the same sense of control when he is offered the opportunity to choose between two types of snacks in the supermarket. We can seize many such opportunities with the young child: Would you like to play on the swings or on the slide? Would you like to have oatmeal or cold cereal for breakfast?

As children get a little older, they can be shown how to read labels and compare products, allowed to make actual purchasing decisions. "Jill picked up a brand of shampoo because she had seen it advertised on television. I asked her to read the label, then to read the label on the supermarket's brand, and compare the prices. We decided it was worth trying the supermarket brand, at least to see if we liked it." Children can learn to weigh advertising claims; they can understand that if the American Dental Association endorses toothpastes with fluoride, then it might be worth buying such toothpaste, while one that claims it makes you "kissable" could be subject to skepticism. School programs are not yet nationwide. But if parents take the time to teach comparison shopping then, when a youngster is ready to assert independence by picking out his own shampoo, he will know how to choose wisely.

Older children can be offered more complex choices, more advanced consumer training. "We narrowed down our new car possibilities to several models, then gave the children a research assignment: pick the best model for us. Jim lost interest right away, but Ted really surprised us. He read all the literature he could get from the car manufacturers, all those fancy brochures. Then he went to the library to look up the consumer magazines. He was very helpful, and we relied heavily on what he found out."

Today's young people spend a lot of money; they will spend more. Consumer education is vital, as essential for the affluent as for the poor. Everyone today has to learn to make decisions, establish priorities, function in the marketplace. Schools can help, and many do, but the fundamental lessons—as in any area that deals with life and living—remain in the hands of parents.

8:

Credit
Where Credit Is Due

If each five- to thirteen-year-old chewed two pieces of gum a week, marketing educator James U. McNeal wrote in 1969, 3,673,200,000 pieces of gum would be consumed per year. At a penny a piece, this mound of gum would cost approximately $36,700,000. And bubble gum, in 1974, went to two cents a piece; "I never thought I'd see the day," my eleven-year-old mourned. With more children, more chewing, and doubled prices, today's outlay for chewing gum must be astronomical.

Give or take a few thousand (million?) dollars spent each year on chewing gum ("Would you parents please ask your children not to chew all day long," a fifth grade teacher pleads on back-to-school night. "I can't make them stop."), the sums involved are but a fragment of a total tapestry: the enormous youth market.

Parents, believe it or not, have the most impact of all on youthful buying habits. Schools, with their consumer education courses, are beginning to have an effect. But we can't ignore another, seemingly all-pervasive, source of influence, the people to whom McNeal was speaking: advertisers. Today's children have so much money, and so much discretion in the ways they choose to spend it (do many parents actually forbid chewing gum? or much else?), that advertisers compete strenuously for each youthful dollar.

"Today's youth are tomorrow's major consumers," Don L. James wrote in *Youth, Media, and Advertising,* a University of Texas marketing study. Some observers might amend that statement to say, "Today's youth are *today's* major consumers." The $27.2 billion that children spent in 1973 may be less than the billions spent by adults—but the youngsters' spending is purely discretionary. It is awesome to comtemplate that much money being spent for nonessentials, for such things as bubble gum and bubble bath.

And the strength of brand loyalty formed in the early years is astounding. A study of brand preferences over many years by Lester Guest of Pennsylvania State University (reported by Eugene Gilbert in *Advertising and Marketing to Young People*) demonstrated how loyalty sticks. In 1940 Dr. Guest surveyed five hundred children from seven to eighteen; some years later fully one-third of the same group, then adults, had the same product preferences. "And those who were eight at the time of the original survey," Gilbert notes, "were as loyal to the brands they had chosen as those who were eighteen."

If marketers can make an impact on teen-agers, that substantial portion of the population which will be the young adults of the next few years, H. Nicholas Windeshausen and Craig G. Clymo wrote in the *University of Washington Business Review* in the spring of 1971, "they can encourage buying behavior and instill corporate identification toward continuing consumption." Marketers know this. Mailbag International, a firm which specializes in offering coupons and/or product samples to college students, thrives on this premise. The object, says president George Schiele, is "to get young people to try products and, we hope, become regular users. The only preference that counts is brand preference."

Young people will try anything that catches their fancy, advertisers say, and the trick, then, is catching their fancy.

There are many techniques. Some rely heavily on pseudo-Freudian psychology. An individual's behavior in the market-place, Philip Kotler writes in the *Journal of Marketing,* is never simple. The shape of a bar of soap has many subtle meanings. A car purchased, its owner claims, for maneuverability may actually have been purchased to convey an image of success, or of aggression. These techniques, of course, are not only directed at children; adults can be victimized by an emotional hard sell too. "You owe your daughter a room like this . . . let us help you to deliver," screams a furniture store newspaper advertisement. "Behold this lovely girl's room—it's an American institution! When your daughter begins to brush her hair and sew flowers on her jeans, the time has come for Daddy to buy her this kind of furniture. For her own private room, of course. . . ."

Then there are the familiar, if blatant, advertising messages: Buy thus-and-so and be kissable, purchase this-and-such and be the very image of success, smoke so-and-so and be athletic. No one, certainly not the average adolescent, no matter what toothpaste, shampoo, shaving cream or cigarettes he uses, can possibly be as attractive as those idealistic images on the tele-vision screen—if anyone takes them seriously. The evidence, as we shall see, indicates that young people are extremely skepti-cal about advertising claims. Yet these claims do have impact. If they did not, advertisers would not enthusiastically spend billions of dollars each year.

The youth market is so large (although the birth rate is dropping) that some corporations are now designing entire department stores just to serve this age group. Not merely a toy store, not solely merchandisers of juvenile furniture, the newest entrepreneurial ventures, like the Kids Kounty stores in Hous-ton, cater to every whim and need of the younger set: furniture, clothing and toys, yes, but also a pet shop, hobby and craft department, photography studio, Scout supplies, candy store, ice cream shop, bicycle sales and repairs. Coming up: party rooms for catered affairs for kids.

"Children are the most easily swayed group of consumers in this country," Melvin Helitzer insists. "They are easily swayed into buying anything. I am frightened at the power we as marketers have over forty million people who in turn influence their parents and others. It becomes easier each year; there is less and less control, authority, discipline each year."

If it is true that there is such a vacuum of parental authority, marketers are doing their best to fill it. Robert Choate, chairman of the Council on Children, Media and Advertising, estimated in 1973 that business may be spending as much as $400,000,000 annually to persuade children or their parents to buy; $164,000,000 of that total is on television messages alone.

Today's youth spend more than 20 percent of all their waking hours with mass media, with television accounting for by far the largest proportion of time. *Changing Times* claimed in 1968 that by the time children graduate from high school they have spent under 11,000 hours in class and over 15,000 hours watching TV. That 15,000 hours could include some 640,000 commercials.

While the average American household has a television set turned on six hours and eighteen minutes a day (whether or not anyone is actually watching), households with children use their TV sets nine hours a week more than the average. "I don't know what my mother did when she had chores she had to get done," a young mother says. "I don't know how I'd manage without the television set." Seventy-eight percent of American families rely on TV, says one study, as an "electronic baby-sitter." Middle-class parents frequently joke, a little bit self-consciously, about using television this way, but appreciate it nonetheless. "The boob tube gives me a quiet hour to prepare dinner," a mother of two preschoolers says. "It's the only way to get those kids out from under my feet."

If you're self-conscious about letting the kids watch too much, consider the statistics. Two- to eleven-year-olds average twenty-three and a half hours a week before the television screen, while twelve- to seventeen-year-olds average nineteen and three-quarters hours. All the studies show a steadily rising curve of television viewing, peaking in the junior high school years at about twenty-five hours a week, then tapering off as teen-agers find other things to do. In other words, addiction isn't necessarily chronic.

These are averages, of course. In general, upper-income families watch less, more education leads to less viewing, and white youngsters are less committed to television than nonwhite. But virtually every American youngster is affected by television to some degree. Parental insistence on abstinence, even to the extreme of not owning a set, doesn't eliminate the influence. One study demonstrated that children who were not allowed to watch any television at all begged their parents, under the influence of their friends who did watch, for TV-advertised toys.

Advertising, in this country, is an integral part of television. The youngest viewers, studies have shown, do not differentiate at all between program content and commercials; the flickering images all look the same. But, with up to twenty-four ads per hour on Saturday morning children's programming, it doesn't take long before the littlest watchers catch the "buy-me" bug.

Fully half of these ads are for food, mostly oversugared cereal and snacks; most of the rest are for toys. Vitamins accounted for 10 percent of children-directed TV advertising until recently; we seem to have finally realized that medicine shouldn't be promoted like candy. (Consumer groups are actively campaigning now for a reduction of sugar-loaded advertising beamed at children.) Youngsters exposed to a constant barrage of ads request the cereals and snacks and toys that look so appealing on the home screen. And middle-class parents are inclined to buy what the child wants.

Charges against the hard sell to children have been circulating since commercial television first began. There's a concise roundup in a technical report issued by the Consumer Research Institute in September 1972. The report, titled "The Effect of Child-Directed TV Advertising on Children," cites the following charges, among others:

1. Claims that a product costs "only" so much play upon a child's ignorance of the relative value of money, and are used

by children in arguing against parental assertions that an item costs too much to buy.

2. Exaggerated advertising claims lead to false expectations and, inevitably, to frustration.

3. Fantasy situations, so often shown in commercials, depict poor reasoning in making product choices. In giving vanity as a valid reason for choice, television also transmits poor values.

4. Commercials contain misrepresentation, exaggeration, fantasy, and deceit; "as the child discovers this, he develops a cynicism not only toward such ads but also toward the free enterprise system, our society, and its institutions."

CRI's report concludes that far more research is needed before these charges can be proved or disproved. Advertisers, needless to say, deny them. "I can't really believe that [advertising to small children] has any real impact on the purchase of the product," Lee Loevinger, a former FCC Commissioner, asserts in *Context*, the DuPont magazine. "Certainly no sensible parent is going to have a four-year-old tell him, 'Daddy, you've got to buy this because I want it.' If the parent is so susceptible that a statement of this sort completely controls his purchase, I don't think anything an advertiser or broadcaster can do is going to have much influence in straightening out that household."

"I wouldn't think of buying all the things Jimmy asks for after he sees them on television," Jimmy's mother says, "but if I'm thinking about a birthday present, why not get him one of the toys he wants?" Jimmy is still very young. The mother of a somewhat older preschooler speaks from experience: "Laurie was so disappointed at the actual size of a doll that looked enormous on the TV screen that we said we'd stay away from advertised toys from now on. They never seem to be quite what the child has been led to expect."

The child, Robert Choate said before the Senate Commerce Committee, "is considered fair game by the country's major advertisers." But studies on the impact of television advertising on youngsters point, above all, to disbelief. "Students' attitudes toward advertising are generally negative," Don James writes.

Youngsters appreciate the communications media as a whole, he says, but "their reactions toward advertising manifested, with increasing maturity, an increasing dislike and lack of confidence."

When Scott Ward of the Harvard Business School surveyed more than a thousand youngsters he found rapidly accelerating cynicism, with decreasing attention paid to commercials as the child matures. "Kindergarten students exhibited confusion, but second graders indicated concrete distrust of commercials, often based on experience with advertised products," Dr. Ward writes in *Effects of Television Advertising on Children and Adolescents.* "Fourth graders exhibited distrust for specific commercials and 'tricky' elements of commercials; sixth graders exhibited global mistrust." Where seven-year-olds showed some cynicism toward specific products, a group of eleven-year-olds expressed general cynicism about all commercials. In part, this progression may result as much from the child's overall cognitive development as from any adverse influence of television; eleven-year-olds view the world in a different light than do seven-year-olds, and are capable of making generalizations: If one commercial is misleading, they all are.

Skepticism toward commercial claims may not be such a bad thing. It may be a healthy move toward independent thinking. "The TV says this game is brand new," says a ten-year-old, "but it's just like another game they advertised before."

Quantities of adverse comment about advertising have poured from the pens of social critics over the past few decades, most referring to the materialism, the excessive regard for possessions fostered by TV. One of the harshest statements, going well beyond concern about materialism, was made by historian Henry Steele Commager in *The New York Review of Books* in July 1973. Referring to corruption in government and manipulation of the Constitution, Commager wrote: "None of this would work if the American people had not been corrupted for more than a generation by the kind of advertising which floods all media day and night, and whose essential principle is manipulation and seduction. A society trained to accept the preposterous claims, the deceptions, and the vulgarities of American advertising can perhaps be manipulated into accepting anything."

But do we accept them? If, in fact, children are growing up with increasing skepticism about advertising claims, if, as Ward indicates, family discussion takes precedence over television advertising in the purchasing decisions of adolescents, the situation may not be quite so bleak. Perhaps, in fact, a generation trained to treat hyperbole with disbelief, to disregard exaggerated claims, may be less susceptible to manipulation.

In the end, of course, parents must shape their children's television habits. What young children watch and how long they watch can be controlled by parents. The materialistic demands generated by commercials can, quite simply, be denied.

Families with access to public, noncommercial television are fortunate, both because the program quality is high and because there are no commercial interruptions. But all parents can be selective. And all parents can combat excessive advertising claims. "When my kids were little," a New York mother says, "they were allowed nothing but two half-hour programs a day on public television. Now that they're older, I discourage excessive viewing (which I still think is anything more than an hour a day, except for Friday evenings, my ten-year-old daughter's weekly pleasure) but don't exert so much control over what they watch. They sure know better than to ask for things they see advertised, though; we've laughed off every such request—and now they laugh at ads."

"It's parental responsibility to say no to 'buy-me's' generated by commercials," Frank P. McDonald of Cunningham & Walsh wrote in *Advertising Age* in May 1973. But removing commercials altogether would, he says, create an unreal world for the child who would still, after all, be subject to advertising from radio, from stores, from friends. "More important," says

McDonald, "sooner or later, the child must learn to cope with the sales message that is a basic part of our economic system."

One of the insistent messages of television and, of course, of the society which television reflects, is "enjoy now, pay later." Whatever the product, it seems, manufacturers would be delighted to have you try it—with or without the ready cash to pay for the pleasure. We take this concept so much for granted that it's difficult to believe how relatively recently the concept of widespread consumer credit became acceptable.

Until World War II people worked, accumulated capital, then, when they could afford it, purchased. In her absorbing study of the Depression and its long-lasting impact, *The Invisible Scar*, Caroline Bird writes that, although a few items—notably cars, sewing machines, pianos and encyclopedias—were sold on the installment plan just prior to the Depression, banks generally disapproved of consumer credit. "Spending before earning, they insisted, could only end in disaster."

Individuals agreed. "Debt was a disgrace," Phyllis McGinley wrote in *The New Breed of Parents*. "A mortgage was something to be wiped out with all possible speed, burned in a ritual ceremony. Nowadays mortgages are considered assets, (to) be paid off in a future where sums now owed will presumably have dwindled in purchasing power."

Today, of course, our entire economy seems based on spending before earning. Mortgages are altogether acceptable. So is virtually every other conceivable form of postponing payment. From 1950 to 1972, according to The National Commission on Consumer Finance, the volume of outstanding consumer credit grew from $14.7 billion to $127.3 billion, more than an eight-fold increase. There are more than 400 million credit cards in the United States today, with more being issued each year. Many wallets bulge with credit cards: for gasoline, department stores, supermarket check cashing privileges, entertainment and travel, and the multipurpose bank card. Fully three-quarters of the recently married couples surveyed by Robert Ferber of the University of Illinois enjoy the use of credit cards; some have as many as nine, few have only one.

"Our capitalist system encourages debt to stimulate sales," says a New York marketing executive. "Families are supposed to be constantly in debt. Use the refrigerator . . . then make the payments."

Credit is considered so vital a component of our economy that some now think it a right, not a privilege. Recipients of public assistance were agitating a few years back for the right to have department store charge accounts; it is discriminatory, they said, to deny them credit.

With credit an integral part of the American Way of Life, it can be difficult to live on cash. Newspapers gleefully reported the recent incident when a distinguished American statesman, arriving back in this country with a pocketful of dollars but no credit cards, was denied car-rental privileges at a Washington airport; his government credentials did him no good. It's an oft-repeated joke, a joke that bears examination, that certain stores will gladly accept a credit card—but ask for identification (!) if you produce cash. Fifteen years ago Tiffany's startled a pair of middle-class newlyweds exchanging a wedding present for a more expensive item by urging them to open a charge account instead of paying the sixteen-dollar difference in cash; they had hardly thought Tiffany's would be interested in charging a sixteen-dollar item—or in encouraging their business. Marilyn Bender spins an amusing tale in *McCall's* magazine about her self-imposed deprivation of credit cards; a month spent living on cash was so frustrating that she went on a credit-card binge when the month was over.

There's no doubt that credit is convenient. As Marilyn Bender found, it's great to have charge privileges when you suddenly come across the desk you've wanted for years, or the perfect dress, or needed garden equipment. It's great not to have to carry large amounts of cash. And, as the distinguished statesman also found, credit is a substantial asset when you travel; without a charge card, Ms. Bender had to pay for a hotel room in advance.

There's equally little doubt that some people can't cope with credit; the obverse side of convenience is danger. Carried away by the affluent society, mesmerized by tantalizing advertising promises, they wind up head over heels in debt. Charge accounts can convey the notion, to the unwary, of temporarily unlimited purchasing power. Poor and affluent alike can fall victim to the temptation of easy credit. And there are more victims around than most people realize. The evidence: proliferating debt-counseling centers. The Consumer Credit Counseling Service of Greater New York, one of about one hundred fifty similar nonprofit agencies in the United States which offer advice, not loans, finds that its charge-happy customers have incomes ranging from $5,200 to $50,000; high incomes do not, by any means, insure ability to cope with credit. Children are subject to the same societal pressures, augmented by the implication that buying on credit confers adult status; can we teach them to handle what so many adults cannot?

"Today's teen-ager," Philip R. Cateora writes in *An Analysis of the Teen-Age Market*, "unlike his depression-conditioned parents, knows prosperity and the rewards of economic opulence." Conditioned by a child-oriented society, accustomed to affluence, he sees no reason to wait for the good things in life. "There's no other country in the world where a kid can graduate from high school and immediately buy a fancy car, rent an apartment with a swimming pool and buy a color TV—all on credit," says Bob M. Gunn, executive director of Credit Counseling Center of Oklahoma. "Kids who marry think they've got to start where their parents are after twenty-five years of marriage and earning. They start in the hole—and some of them never get out of it." Too many young couples, even well-educated ones, are in debt almost from the beginning. With too-easy credit they buy expensive appliances, furniture, cars, and wind up with damaged budgets, damaged credit ratings and, sometimes, damaged marriages.

The *1970 Survey of Consumer Finances*, by the University of Michigan's Survey Research Center, reports that slightly less than half of all American families had outstanding installment debt in the first part of 1970. More than two-thirds of families in the twenty-five to thirty-four age group had some outstanding debt. Ten percent of families in this age group and 16 percent of families whose heads are under twenty-five lay out at least one-fifth of gross annual income on installment debt payments. The future apparently looks rosy to young families, so rosy that many of them appear willing, even eager, to mortgage it in advance. In an era of affluence, say sociologists, people live well and expect to continue to live well. They see no need to worry about a future that will take care of itself.

Familiarity with the idea of deferred payment sometimes starts early. "My mother doesn't like me to carry a lot of money around," a Manhattan fifth grader explains. "So when I eat lunch at the luncheonette near school, I charge it and my mother pays the bill." The only problem with this approach is that, as far as the youngster is concerned, money has no place in the transaction. *He* doesn't pay the bill, he doesn't have to be particularly concerned with monthly totals. As a convenience for parent and child, charging lunches is great; as a lesson in the use of credit, it is missing a component.

Familiarity, although not necessarily comprehension, grows as the child grows, as he sees his parents function in a cashless society. Whip out a credit card and pay for the fourth grader's back-to-school wardrobe; flash a courtesy card and cash a check in the supermarket for the weekly groceries. Few parents take the time to explain to youngsters how all these pieces of paper and celluloid cards take the place of money, but the idea does sink in somehow. By the time children enter high school, many have at least a nodding personal acquaintance with credit.

Eight hundred fifty thousand teen-age girls, *Seventeen* magazine reported, have their own personal charge accounts; another 5.5 million (or 44.4 percent of the total) have the use of their mother's charge accounts. *Consumer Reports,* in September 1972, claimed that 19 percent of all fourteen- to eighteen-year-olds had department store credit cards. And a 1972 survey by Louis Harris indicated that 20 percent of eighteen- to twenty-year-olds hold bank credit cards—compared to 54 percent of the adult population.

While a banker recently stated that "kids today are not convinced that paying cash is important," Aaron Cohen, Research Director of *Seventeen* magazine, is not so sure. "Kids today may be a little more wary of credit than adult society. They feel they don't need everything, they can wait a little. There will always be a core of those who want things in a hurry, expensive things, what they want when they want it," Cohen says, "but they're not necessarily representative of the whole." Philip Cateora found that the high school students he studied agreed that credit is necessary but that it should be used sparingly and with extreme caution. "It's okay to use credit," one of his respondents said, "but just remember you're not getting something for nothing." Perhaps some teens are innately conservative—or afraid of themselves. "I wouldn't want my own charge," a fifteen-year-old girl said emphatically. "You would spend like crazy—and then realize you wouldn't be able to pay."

But retailers who have tried granting limited credit to teen-agers report generally favorable results. "These little kids will charge a $27.50 ring," a jeweler says, "and come in faithfully each week to pay back part of the bill." So-called "junior accounts," usually offered by neighborhood merchants rather than by large institutions, are frequently limited to $25 or $50.

While most large credit grantors and banks stay clear of the younger set (insisting that all applicants regardless of age meet standard criteria: steady income, ability to pay, and good previous credit record), Valley National Bank in Phoenix is one institution that has made an all-out effort to attract teen-agers. If a student has a regular savings account, maintains a checking account, and attends a series of money-management classes, he is given a bank credit card with a nominal credit line. If the high schooler handles this limited credit satisfactorily, the line of credit is expanded. The bank's goal: adult credit customers who know how to manage money. While Valley National Bank and other groups who grant credit to young people feel strongly that they are teaching a valuable lesson in money management, others feel equally strongly that the lesson is misplaced when aimed at the young. The President of New York's Bowery Savings Bank, testifying before a Senate subcommittee a few years ago, compared extending credit to youngsters to teaching them to use narcotics.

Many parents are wary too. "It's wrong for teens to charge," says one New Jersey woman whose four children range from twelve to twenty. "When you handle money, you get a feel for money. Charging distorts that feeling. When you use a card, you just don't get the sense of it." A California mother agrees; charge card in hand, her fourteen-year-old daughter bought two dresses without even trying them on. They didn't fit. The store took them back, but if it hadn't, the daughter would have had to pay. Record and book clubs, according to Consumers Union, are a major trap for teen-agers. But, used with discretion by mature teens, they can be okay. "I just allowed my daughter to join a book club," says a father who disapproves of teen credit. "We carefully explained that she would be responsible for buying a certain number of books and that she would have to pay the bill when it arrives. She's a realist, and she'll put money away to pay the bills, but I'll keep an eye on it."

Too often, whether the credit used by a youngster is in his own name or in his parent's, it is the parent who takes ultimate responsibility for paying the bills. He has the legal responsibility, of course, when a child is under eighteen, as well as an understandable parental desire to keep his offspring out of trouble, but some effort should be made to teach the fundamental credit lesson that the piper must be paid, bills must be taken care of. "My daughter says 'thanks for the credit card, Dad'" one father complains, "and thinks she's squared accounts."

The problem can be more severe when interfamily loans are granted and there is no outside agency to send a bill. "I've got a hunch that kids are learning the worst possible lessons about earning, saving, borrowing and capitalism," says Melvin Hel-

itzer. "Children, with few sources of funds, want instant gratification, so they borrow from their parents. Parents want to be
loved, so they agree to the loan. Junior wants to buy a second-
hand car, for instance, so he borrows three hundred dollars from
Dad and agrees to pay back ten dollars a week. It lasts for three
or four weeks and then Junior says 'oh, come on, Dad'—and
that's it. Kids get away with this because we're overindulgent.
But these kids, in debt but not responsible to pay the debt, are
going to be hard-pressed to adjust to financial responsibility if
and when they have to."

The day of reckoning dawns a little earlier now that the age
of majority is eighteen. High school students who have turned
eighteen are not only eligible to vote they are, in many states,
legally entitled to enter into contracts and incur debt, legally
responsible for themselves. Many are not prepared. "New
Adults Surprised," says a headline about Connecticut's
lowered legal age, "They Must Pay Piper."

While most credit grantors may be loathe to grant credit to
the average eighteen-year-old, requiring first that he hold a
steady job, college students, even when unemployed, seem such
a potentially desirable market that their immediate lack of
income can be ignored. Asserting that statistics prove college
students to be a good credit risk, Irvin Penner, president of
Gracious Lady Services and its College Credit Card Corporation division, told members of the National Retail Merchants
Association to get out there and grant them credit. If we deny
them credit, he said, we are denying them one of the major
symbols of maturity and adulthood, and telling them they are
not worthy of the system's faith or confidence. Furthermore,
it's a lucrative and ever-increasing market, one retailers would
be foolish to ignore.

True enough, many banks and corporations are eager to tap
the college market. Unsolicited credit-card invitations appear
in campus mailboxes with almost the frequency with which
they appear in yours and mine. But are college students
equipped to manage this new-found financial glory, any better
equipped than their younger brothers and sisters?

Many college students are being forced to face debt, debt that may not seem so glorious, by the rapidly escalating cost of college itself. Fewer families, even upper-middle-income families, can manage college costs on their own, especially if more than one child is off to school at once. The answer, in more and more cases: student loans. Debt, in these cases, can be a shock. One Harvard student, borrowing to pay for room and board, was quoted in *The New York Times* as saying he's not quite sure how much he owes: "It's a little bit like calculating the distance between stars. The numbers are so astronomical they don't mean anything."

There isn't much that can cushion this shock. But consumer credit in the form of department store charge accounts and bank charge cards is another matter. Just as parents take pains to introduce children to money management through the vehicle of allowances, as they introduce the youngster to banking through his own bank account, so they can—and should—round out the experience by teaching about credit, its advantages and disadvantages. The first lessons are learned by example, as children shop with parents and see parents cope with the resulting bills, but the college years are a reasonable time to introduce a youngster to his own personal credit. "We opened accounts for Susan in the college bookstore, and in a local clothing store when she went off to school," the mother of a nineteen-year-old says. "She had a budget for clothing for the year, which we placed in her checking account, and it seemed reasonable for her to charge purchases and handle the bills herself. It's worked out satisfactorily; she hasn't abused the privilege of charging because she knows she's getting the bills, not us."

The intricacies of credit must be made crystal clear, however. "We pointed out to Susan," this mother goes on, "that if she paid her bills promptly she wouldn't have to pay extra in finance charges. It's so easy to let them get out of hand." And, as another parent points out, "The kids have to realize that a record is kept of promptness of payment and so on. If a kid is sloppy now, it's going to affect his credit record later on."

Whether or not we approve of the buy-now–pay-later orientation of society, the syndrome seems here to stay. Our children will have to learn to live with it—which doesn't necessarily mean getting caught up and swept away with easy credit. There's little point in our going to the opposite extreme either. We can rely on cash for most purchases, continue fervent belief in the Puritan work ethic, and still find times when a good credit record is essential. To get and maintain such a record takes intelligent money management, starting early.

9:

Rainy Days

Oddly enough, while Americans spend enormous amounts, we are also hooked on saving. Young people as well as adults seem to have the habit. Ninety-three percent of the young people surveyed by the Institute of Life Insurance in 1972 think saving is important; college graduates, far more than in 1970 (perhaps because of recent job uncertainty), believe in regular systematic saving. And *Seventeen* magazine reported near the end of 1973 that twelve and a half million, or 88 percent, of the nation's thirteen- to nineteen-year-old girls have their own savings accounts, up from 63 percent in 1968.

How do young people get the savings habit? And is it a habit parents should stress in teaching money management?

Most of us, brought up on a steady diet of earn, save, then spend, say "yes, saving is a good idea." Firmly convinced of the merits of saving as a virtue in itself, we pass along this conviction to our offspring. One of the first gifts often bestowed on newborns, symbolic though it may be, is a piggy bank. Watch the pennies add up, get the savings habit, be prepared for that rainy day. . . .

Banks, of course, push the savings idea. A little booklet distributed by a New York City savings bank suggests having a preschooler stash his pennies in a glass jar (one he can't open, of course, saving isn't *his* idea) so that he will have the incentive of actually seeing the money mount up. The bank also suggests adding a few cents now and then as "interest" on his savings.

But normal kids, especially little kids, given the option, will spend their money for immediate pleasure. Thoughts for the future belong only to adults. Most young children save their pennies only under duress, at their parents' insistence. "Half my weekly allowance (of fifty cents) has to be put right in the piggy bank," a third grader reports. "Then, when it adds up, my mother takes it to the real bank. She says it's for me, but I can't ever use it. Money in the bank is stuck; it never comes out."

There's little rhyme or reason to saving, as far as small children can tell. Those pennies cascading into the painted pig make a satisfying plunk only to the parents' ears; Junior knows only that they disappear, never to be seen again. He can't comprehend large sums; pennies mean more then quarters for a long time. He has to mature before he can grasp the glory of magnified money. And, more important, he has little concept of time, up to age six or seven, and has trouble visualizing tomorrow; saving for a future he cannot understand simply has no meaning. "It took me years to understand what my father was talking about when he said to save for a rainy day," recalls a supermarket manager. "I always thought it was more fun to spend money when it was sunny outside."

Generally, an adult has savings goals. They may be as specific as next summer's vacation or a new car, or as long-range as graduate school for the toddler or retirement income for the young father; the thought may be simply to provide a financial cushion in case of emergency. But sights are set on *something*. Despite the Puritan concept that saving is virtuous and thrift is noble, people, most people, willingly save only for a reason. A young child lives very much in the present; it's today that counts. This is normal. Tell him he's getting a new baby brother or sister in six months and he'll either ignore the whole thing or ask you every day if it's time yet. Tell him he's saving money for future education and he won't know what you're talking about. Until he's nine or ten or even twelve he'll have trouble planning ahead. And until he can plan ahead, visualize the future, he can't understand the concept of deferred gratification—which is what saving is all about, depriving yourself of something today so that you'll have something better tomorrow.

Yet parents, many parents, convinced that it's the only way to teach children the advantages of saving, often insist that children save. In some families a designated portion of the weekly allowance must be immediately set aside—a practice which effectively reduces the allowance. Frequently, too, monetary gifts are appropriated by parents, in whole or in part, and banked. What good is a birthday present, thinks the child, if it's in one hand and out the other, with never the least chance to spend it? "I wish Grandma would give me a toy. If she gives me money, it's not a present at all."

While it's often easier for adults to give cash than to find something that would be really appreciated by overgifted youngsters, while many adults sincerely believe that youngsters prefer cash, it can turn out to be no gift at all. Grandma wants Junior to buy something for himself, but he doesn't know what he wants either. "I can't let him fritter away ten dollars on bowling," says Mother, "so he has to put it in the bank until there's something special he wants." Maybe bowling would be special to the child, but he doesn't get to choose. And once in the bank often means gone forever; the money gets "stuck."

If Junior really would rather have money, perhaps we ought to ask why. If it helps him in his long-range efforts to secure a microscope or a bicycle or whatever, if he will use it for bowling or ice-skating, fine. But if it's money for money's sake, it's another story. Then, if we stimulate this kind of money-consciousness, encourage it by monetary gifts, we shouldn't mind when it's reversed. "Joe gave us five dollars for our anniversary," says his mother, a little chagrined at this eleven-year-old's being so sure his parents would like money as a gift—but also a little bit proud that he was so "adult" as to think of giving cash.

We overemphasize money as an object in itself when we stress saving, accumulation, hoarding. "If you save half your allowance, I'll match your savings," a father offers as incentive. But what is the child supposed to be saving *for?* Endlessly talking about college through the grade school years may dim its luster by the time the child really wants to think about it. "I earned about ten dollars a week last summer, when I did two paper routes," says a thirteen-year-old, "but I had to bank most of it. My folks said it was for college. But I needed the money last summer."

It's not a bad idea to inculcate the idea that money saved today, not frittered away, can be spent for something more impressive tomorrow. It's not a bad idea to encourage children to save. But trying too hard, too soon, can be counterproductive. It simply doesn't do much good. A kindergartner just can't be expected to save at all. An eight- or nine-year-old may be ready to plan three or four weeks ahead, to put off buying bubble gum and save for a set of plastic cowboys. This is an opportune time, when he wants something more expensive than his allowance can provide, to point out what saving can accomplish. Enthusiasm is more easily generated when there is a short-term, manageable goal. And the idea of saving is more likely to take root and flourish when the child himself wants something: plastic cowboys, perhaps, or, when he's older, a new bike, a dog, a summer hosteling trip, a season pass to the school games. . . . Whatever it is, real motivation must come from inside. Even then you have to expect periodic backsliding, especially with younger children; the temptation of a candy bar or a comic book in the here and now may override the desired cowboys still a month (an eternity) away.

The older a youngster gets, the more his time sense stretches, so that he can save over a period of time unimaginable—and intolerable—to a younger child. A junior high school student might voluntarily save all winter for a baseball mitt for spring practice, but he too might take one step backward for every two steps forward and need a great deal of parental encouragement to keep to his goal. If a youngster has zealously saved for months, an unexpected gift—a dollar or two from parents or grandparents—might renew his flagging interest. The important thing, however, in every case, is self-motivation; even older adolescents won't want to save without a reason. "My father could never convince me that saving was any good until I wanted to go skiing and didn't have any money," says a sixteen-year-old with a passion for skiing. "Now I save all my baby-sitting money and I'm getting a Saturday job in a dry cleaner's so I can go skiing more often. I want to ski in Europe next year."

And that raises another question: Should she be allowed to go skiing or should her earnings be saved for college? Many parents would insist that all or a substantial part of her earnings should go toward college, if indeed she wants further education. But should money lie in the bank, dedicated to college, while parents foot the bill for other things? This particular family would never send their daughter skiing, and certainly not to Europe, unless she earned her way. But what about other expenses? Should parents pay for sports equipment, band instruments, summer camp—while the child's earnings all go in the bank, sacred to the principle of saving? "We let Jeff use his earnings for his regular expenses; we put away all we can toward college." "Well," says another, "we think Jim should have the sense of contributing toward his own education. It should mean more to him then. I'd rather pay some of his expenses now."

Purpose is the determining factor. What does the child want to do? Gail's motivation for that dry-cleaning job is her desire to ski. Pre-empting her earnings for college might, in depriving her of setting her own goals and working toward them, take away all her desire to work. In another adolescent, college might be the overriding motivation. "We told Lee that she could live at home and go to a community college absolutely free," a Maryland father explains, "but if she wanted to go away from home, she had to pay half the freight. She lived at home and went to the local college for two years, working in a dress shop until she earned enough to contribute two thousand dollars a year toward college."

Once youngsters have the desire to save, for plastic cowboys, ski trips, or college, it will be reinforced by your example. Attitudes are not transmitted in lecture format. When children see that parents put money aside, postpone pleasures, have plans and goals, both long-range and short, they get the idea. "Watching you save, or doing it together," according to New York psychiatrist Lisa Tallal, "teaches delayed gratification in contrast to instant gratification, a sign of maturity. Babies can't wait; older people can."

At times, in saving as in other areas, parents are inconsistent. "My father said he would match whatever we earned," says a sixteen-year-old, "but when we got up to twenty dollars he cut it out." And a thirteen-year-old New Jersey boy complains: "My mother tells me to save. Then she borrows my money to pay for groceries after she spends her own on pocketbooks. She's always buying pocketbooks." These all-too-human inconsistencies shouldn't, since these parents otherwise set a thrifty example, have any ill effect beyond annoyance.

If example doesn't provide a spur to saving, if there is no inner motivation, no personal desire to postpone and thereby enlarge pleasure, saving has to be forced. And when it is, the stress is on accumulation, on money for its own sake rather than for what it can do. "My eleven-year-old gets money from us if he behaves himself, and if he minds his little sister," says a European-born hairdresser, an authoritarian father. "But he's not allowed to spend much. When he accumulates a little, I put it in the bank for him. When the bank account gets up to eighteen dollars and seventy-five cents it goes for a savings bond. He keeps track of the interest, cashes the bonds after five years, buys more, and puts the difference in the bank again. I tell him we never know what the future will bring so we have to be prepared and not spend money. He's very conscious of money already, and of the interest he earns." He's so conscious, in fact, that his main joy in money lies in counting it, not necessarily a healthy concept for an eleven-year-old.

It's much healthier for children to learn to use money, to spend wisely, psychiatrists claim, than to hoard and never spend. It's much easier to convince a person who knows how to spend that he can do better by waiting a bit and buying something bigger than it is to convince a compulsive hoarder to spend at all. Parents should exercise caution and, while teaching that money should be spent with care, avoid teaching that it's better not to spend it at all. A school psychologist in Connecticut tells of an unhappy fourteen-year-old who has learned this lesson too well. She has saved seven hundred dollars of her baby-sitting money toward college, but knows nothing at all about spending. When she wanted to buy her mother a birthday present she floundered with not the least idea what things cost or how to shop. "She squeezes the dollar," says the psychologist, "it's a mystical thing to her. But it would be better if she understood money as a practical tool, something to be used in daily life, not something which exists for itself alone."

We all know adults pathologically unable to spend, compulsive about saving. Normally, writes psychoanalyst Edmund Bergler in *Money and Emotional Conflicts,* money is a means to an end, used for acquiring desired objects; neurotically, money is an end in itself. "Normally," he goes on, "the spending of money is taken for granted; it needs no surgical operation to put a dollar into circulation. Neurotically, the possession and hoarding of money becomes the predominant motif." It's better, say psychologists, to let children get the feel of spending, to learn the practical uses of money, even through making mistakes, than to induce extreme caution about spending. Consider your child's inherent temperament. If he is an extrovert who distributes money wildly, he may have to be curbed. If he is a cautious youngster, reluctant to spend, insecure in making a purchasing decision, encourage him to spend rather than to save endlessly. "I save all my money," says ten-year-old Valerie. "I just like to save." Irrational hoarding is fairly common at this age; it need not be encouraged. Valerie would be better off learning to spend, to derive pleasure from what money can provide. Children who learn this lesson, who learn what money can and cannot do, are less likely to go to extremes as adults, less likely to use money for emotional reasons.

While children should learn to spend, many parents prefer to limit the amounts they have to play with. This poses a problem when grandparents are generous or Junior starts earning substantial amounts—and at this point, if not before, bank savings accounts are frequently urged upon children. When the children are quite young, in fact, parents often take grandparental gifts and deposit them in the bank, with the children none the wiser. When the children are a bit older and know about the gift—after all, Grandma wants recognition— tactics have to change. Few parents, today, feel comfortable being completely arbitrary about what the child may spend or must save; this is the time for diplomacy and a good time to encourage savings. "The children opened their own savings accounts a couple of years ago," says a Pennsylvania mother whose daughter and son are eight and twelve. "If they got a check from a grandparent, we would suggest that they keep a few dollars and save the rest; they soon learned to go to the bank, themselves, and make the deposit. It gives them a grown-up feeling." And because they bank for themselves they don't feel that their parents are arbitrarily appropriating their money.

Dr. Yudowitz feels that parents and children should nego- tiate what is to be done with cash presents. "There should be rules, rules are good for children, but they should be involved in the development of the rules." They should discuss not only what portion of a gift goes into the bank but when withdrawals may be made.

Often, when parents bank money for their children, the children themselves have a very hazy idea of what happens to the money. "My boys got very upset when we told them the bank uses their money," reports an Ohio mother. "They thought if it was their money, the bank should keep it separate and not touch it." And another parent remembers vividly how distressed her child was when a withdrawal was made: "He got fives instead of the singles he had deposited and was convinced that it wasn't his money at all, that the bank had done something dreadful with his money." Dr. Yudowitz says: "Don't put the child's money in the bank for him. Take him with you, involve him in the process, and explain just what happens. The mechanics of banking are fascinating to a child, if they're explained to him. It's good to get across the concept of a nest egg, a storehouse, a root cellar—but you have to involve the child in the whole process, not just take his money away in the name of saving."

Even children involved in the process often remain confused for a while. "Danny wants two accounts," says his father, "one to spend, one to save. He thinks five percent interest and four percent interest add up." Despite the suggestion that adding pennies to the preschooler's glass jar may convey the idea of interest, it is far more likely that children will begin to understand the concept after they reach fifth or sixth grade, learn percentages, and see why the bank should pay for the use of their money. When youngsters learn what banks do with depositors' money they learn, gradually, how money is invested, goods produced and distributed, the basics of our economic system. It's a difficult concept to get across, especially if you try too soon. The preschooler, glass jar and all, really won't understand. Some parents try to teach economics by paying interest if they borrow change from their children; others charge interest if and when they grant an advance on allowance. Most prefer to keep bank practices out of family relationships. All that's necessary, really, with a child who's old enough, is an explanation, preferably in concrete terms: "If you put your summer's earnings in the bank, the bank might loan the money to Uncle Al when he wants to buy a car. The bank pays you interest on your savings, pays you for the privilege of using your money for the car loan, and Uncle Al pays interest to the bank for the use of the money."

School savings plans, highly touted in much of the country since their inception in Long Island City in 1885, are supposed to mold good habits of thrift; they don't, unless handled exceptionally well, teach anything much about banking and economics. They may not necessarily even teach much about thrift. Too often, they are simply forced savings, forced in two ways: because the parents think it's a good idea and because of the psychological pressure of keeping up with classmates and meeting teacher expectations. It's a terrible moment when a seven-year-old has to say, "No, Miss Smith, I didn't bring any money for the bank today." And whose money is the child saving? The parent who gives Johnny money for the bank each week, with the best of intentions, is not really teaching him anything about saving, about deferring gratification for himself, nothing more, in fact, than the parent who insists that half of each allowance goes promptly into a piggy bank. If the child has an allowance, or earns money, that is the money that should be used for piggy bank or school savings—when and if the child wants to save. Until the motivation comes from within, the lesson will not be learned. "Saving," said Sidonie Matsner Gruenberg, former director of the Child Welfare League of America, "is not a habit that can be forced upon an individual. It's a way of thinking and feeling."

But banks, and parents, continue to push saving, banks out of self-interest, parents because it's "good for the children."

Yet, apart from school savings plans, banks vary considerably in their policies toward junior-grade savings. Although the law permits bank accounts to be maintained by minors, some banks prefer a parent as trustee. "You don't want him taking money out of the account," explains one suburban savings bank officer to a parent trying to open an individual account for her twelve-year-old son. "We suggest that you keep it a trust account, even though it's his earnings, at least until he's sixteen." And a New York City banker states categorically: "We try to discourage single-name accounts before the child is sixteen; he could withdraw money and the bank would be held responsible—the parents could even bring us into court."

Most banks will open an account solely for a child as soon as he can sign his name, if the parent insists, but can be very persuasive in convincing the parent to retain control. "We don't have a minimum age for savings accounts," I was told by bank after bank. "It's up to the parents' judgment whether the child is competent to manage money. But we suggest that few children under fifteen or sixteen are really competent." While school savings plans will accept children who can only print their names, most banks prefer signatures in script—usually, then, the child is at least seven or eight years old. Signatures, in these cases, should be frequently updated. "When I tried to withdraw funds from an account opened as a child, I had a devil of a time with the bank," a young woman notes. "They kept saying my signature wasn't the same, and I kept saying that I wasn't eight years old anymore."

Some banks, however, urge children to open their own accounts. Some have full-scale promotions aimed at children. A bank in Dubuque, Iowa, has had a successful Junior Savers Program for the past twelve years, complete with an annual theater party for junior savers, including free popcorn, prizes, and gifts—an event, the bank says, which "stimulates a great deal of enthusiasm among the junior bankers." Every new parent in Dubuque receives a letter from the bank (along with letters, no doubt, from diaper-service solicitors and photographers); when parents deposit ten dollars in an account for a newborn the bank adds one dollar as an incentive. Most of these accounts are trust accounts, but the bank welcomes an eight or nine-year-old who walks in and requests an account for himself alone.

In Colorado one bank sponsors free Saturday morning movies for children who present their savings passbooks to get a movie ticket. No passbook, no ticket; no ticket, no movie. Deposits are not mandatory, but once in the bank, passbook in hand, many youngsters add to their accounts.

These banks are trying to hook savers early; children's accounts are usually peanuts (in fact, many banks no longer maintain school savings plans because they cost more than they bring in), but bankers know that sheer inertia will probably keep customers banking in the same place for years to come. "We have instances in which the first exposure was a child's savings account and eventually the individual used our facilities for the purchase of a home, or an investment in a business," says Thomas H. Kelly II, Vice-President of Northwestern Bank in Owatonna, Minnesota. "We are extremely conscious of young people, for they are the entire future of the banking industry."

What about the accounts parents open for their children? What happens when the children become old enough to handle banking for themselves? Some parents let the children take over, merging college funds saved by parents with the children's earnings. "We handled all their banking until they reached eleven or twelve," says a father of six, "then they each took over, banking gifts and earnings. Having a large family helps, I think. First of all, they benefit from seeing what the older ones have accomplished with their savings. And secondly, they know that we can't supply everything for this many children; they have to save for themselves." Most parents, though, large families or small, keep separate accounts. "We have college trust accounts for the children, but they have their own for their personal savings, their earnings and gifts from grandparents. They get a kick out of watching the interest mount up on their personal funds. And if they want to buy something big, like a ten-speed bicycle, they can tap their accounts; the college fund is inviolate."

As children reach the teens they should be encouraged, but still not forced, to save. Meanwhile, there are several ways parents can bank for children. You can, of course, just open a bank account in your own name and mentally designate it for the child's benefit. But then you have to pay income tax on the interest; depending on your tax bracket it could be a hefty chunk. You also have to have the willpower to keep it a separate account.

Then there are joint accounts, which can be established for parent and child as for husband and wife. They offer no tax benefits and parents must recognize that the child, as a joint owner, could withdraw all the money. Because of this, many banks limit these accounts and will not allow a youngster as a joint tenant unless he is at least sixteen. This, too, varies from bank to bank: one says not till sixteen, another says when the child is of legal age, and still another leaves it up to the parent. "We point out the risk, that the child can take out all the money. If the parent responds, 'That's okay, it's his money,' we'll open the account. If he says, 'Oh, he wouldn't do that,' we strongly suggest a trust account."

If you open a custodial account, under your state's Uniform Gifts to Minors Act, the youngster can't touch the money until he's of legal age. The major advantage, however, is that interest is taxable to the child, not to you; since he's unlikely to be earning much in the way of taxable income this feature can represent considerable tax savings. The child must have a social security number, easily obtained from any Social Security office, no matter how young he is when you open the account. Parents, and grandparents too, says one banker, should take advantage of the tax benefits available when interest on a child's bank account, or on corporate dividends, are reported to the child's social security number. But, again, banks vary. Another banker told me that custodial accounts are very complicated; he recommends them only when substantial amounts are involved.

Trust accounts are far more common. Here you pay the taxes but you also retain control throughout your own lifetime (unless you choose to terminate the trust); the child assumes control of the funds upon the death of the trustee.

One banking area that remains a mystery to many young people, and not a few older ones as well, is checking, although *Seventeen* magazine did find that 23.9 percent of teen-age girls (most of them over seventeen) had checking accounts in 1973, up from 12.8 percent in 1968. Yet few youngsters handle checking accounts before they go off to college or enter the business world; many don't write their first check until they're married. Then checks can be oddly confused with long-range credit. "It just didn't seem as if I was spending money by writing checks," a not atypical young man confesses. And an attorney, mother of two, recalls: "I had a checking account in college that taught all the wrong lessons. I still suffer from it. I knew it was an extension of my father's account and I could write all the checks I wanted and no one said a word. I walked around a hundred and fifty dollars overdrawn—and my father was just pleased that I bought books." Whenever that first checking account is opened, for college or with marriage, neither high school diploma nor wedding license confers automatic financial know-how; people must be taught how to use checking accounts, preferably before they abuse them.

One father, a Denver accountant, has strong feelings on the subject. After seeing too many clients with no concept of how to handle money he determined to do better by his sons; he gave each a personal checking account on his twelfth birthday. "It's a learning tool, like an allowance," he says. "I deposit enough money in the accounts to cover tuition, medical bills, dentistry, as well as whatever they need for sports and entertainment; then the boys pay all the bills." There was a little difficulty at first, as local merchants were reluctant to accept a check signed by a twelve-year-old—and the boys themselves discovered it was wiser to keep quiet about it with their friends—but the whole family agrees that it worked out well. The boys learned what medical insurance was all about—and when one of them was hospitalized after he inhaled a pen top, he learned what it costs for hospitalization over and above insurance. And, says the other boy's orthodontist, "He wore his retainer more faithfully than any other patient I've ever had; he was paying the bills and wanted to stop doing so as soon as possible."

This system isn't likely to work for all families. Few parents would consider giving their twelve-year-olds—or their four-teen-year-olds—checking accounts. And few banks want to open checking accounts for teen-agers. "A checking account is a matter of need, when you have bills to pay," says one banker, speaking for many. "What would be the point of a teen-ager having one?" The accountant father looks upon checking accounts as a learning tool for his sons, on a larger scale than pocket money. Few bankers agree. One of the largest New York banks says flatly: no checking account until eighteen. Some will consider the younger teen-ager who is working and has bills to pay, if he seems responsible. "If a paper boy has accounts to pay, we would open a checking account for him, but it's not a plaything," says one bank officer. "We would have to see a reason." Bank policy varies so much—there is no uniform national law, or national policy—that parents who like this idea may be able to find a receptive banker.

Banks that do consider high school students with earned income appropriate candidates for checking accounts sometimes limit them to special accounts, more costly than regular accounts. One savings bank which does offer a regular account insists on a minimum balance of one hundred dollars with young customers; its accounts for older customers are completely free with no required minimum. But many of these "free" checking accounts are inextricably linked with backup credit; the account is only free because if it is overdrawn an automatic loan comes into play. The assumption, of course, is that the bank makes back its money on the loans, for which regular interest is charged. Even if the loan provision is never used, the holder of such an account must meet credit requirements; not many adolescents, even those with earned income, can do so. One large New York bank insists on credit references for an ordinary checking account, references that might be difficult for a high school student to secure—although the bank points out that an active savings account is in the applicant's favor.

Some banks try to entice the college market. One institution that will reluctantly open a checking account for a high school student, requiring a minimum balance, goes overboard to lure college depositors: free checking, half-price traveler's checks, and an almost-guaranteed loan of up to $1,500. "We want them to bank with us when they finish college," an officer says.

It's a good idea for parents to give high school students some experience with checking, some practical knowledge of what it's all about, before they go off to college or full-time employment, before they are lured by free checking and easy credit they can't quite handle. After all, it's been years since checks were tools of the very rich; almost all middle-class American families have checking accounts as a matter of course. So will these young people. They should know what they're doing. One possibility might be handling the quarterly or semester allowance for a high school junior or senior, a youngster who should be handling most of his own expenses anyway, through a checking account. That way, the youngster can learn how to handle checks, how to balance his books while he's still at home under parental supervision and receiving parental guidance. But the parent should be careful, suggests a Boston banker, that he doesn't force the issue; there should be some enthusiasm on the youngster's part.

Banking is with us to stay. Cash, some say, will be used less and less as checks and easy credit take over. Saving, postponing pleasure, deferring gratification to make it bigger and better, will remain a fundamental precept for most families. Introduce children to saving, but don't force them; don't make them compulsive about money. Saving can be negative, a denial of the self, or it can be what we want it to be, something positive, a temporary postponement of good things. With children, and with ourselves, we should emphasize the positive.

10:

The Great Rip-Off

There's a little larceny in us all, it's been said—and sometimes it seems to go double for children. Almost every youngster has, at least once, appropriated something he shouldn't have. You may hear about it first from his best friend's mother, or from a neighborhood storekeeper, or you may become suspicious at some shiny new toy he's flashing—but when it happens, you're not alone.

Shoplifting almost has a place in American folklore: along with turning over outhouses and plucking fruit in a forbidden orchard goes swiping candy from the five-and-dime or an apple from the neighborhood fruit stand. Parents, many with personal memories of such activities, either panic when they first realize that that new plaything was not come by honestly —after all, it's up to parents, fond memories or not, to instill moral rectitude in their offspring—or they pass it all off as a joke. Neither response is always appropriate. What is appropriate depends on the age of the child and the frequency of incidence.

Without belittling shoplifting as an offense—it has reached

horrifying proportions among adolescents, and we shall discuss that problem in a moment—there's not too much point in panic when a small child "borrows" an attractive item. It seldom implies any serious personality disturbance—or any disturbance at all—when a toddler, or for that matter a child of eight, takes something once.

Very little children simply have no concept of property; it's one of the basic parental tasks, in our noncommunal culture, to teach them the difference between "mine" and "thine." But we must be realistic and understand that the lesson takes awhile to penetrate, with much backsliding along the way. Small children will pick up coins from Daddy's dresser the same way they pick up a cookie. They just have no idea that it's wrong, or that money has any especial value. You may want to stop them, not only because it's terribly inconvenient not to have the bus fare handy when you need it but also because you want them to know for the long run that it's not an issue to get terribly upset about. In fact, if you do, it may attach too much importance to money as an object. We want our children to value money, but not to over-value it.

It isn't always money that little ones acquire. I once returned from an errand to the housewares store, when my son was under two, and found his stroller stashed with nightlights, neatly fixed to their cardboard backings. This was no more "stealing" than his picking up coins from the dresser, although it certainly merited—and received—a quick trip back to the store to return the merchandise.

An under-two was probably not conscious of what he was doing. The three-and-a-half-year-old who lifted some little-girl cosmetics from the drugstore counter, however, did know; "I need them," she protested when her mother removed the "lipstick" from her grip. That doesn't mean she understood that taking them was wrong. Even three- and four-year-olds who have developed a rudimentary notion of private property (at least when it comes to their own belongings—"You can't play with that truck, it's mine!") will pick up things that look attractive, whether it's another child's toy (the principle doesn't apply in reverse), a roll of tape from the stationery store, or a pencil left by the kitchen telephone.

As they get a little older temptation is balanced, sometimes, by the knowledge that taking things is wrong. Occasionally temptation wins—to be followed immediately by contrition. "When David was in first grade," his mother reports, "he took something from a local bookstore. He got outside, couldn't stand it, and immediately said, 'Look what someone gave me.' I said, 'Think hard, while I stand here on the sidewalk.' He marched right back inside and told the man he was sorry."

As the child approaches eight, say Frances L. Ilg and Louise Bates Ames in *Child Behavior,* he becomes vividly aware of money and what it can buy. Although by this time he knows better, at least in theory, temptation may be too strong. So it's sometimes best, in these early years, to remove temptation around the house, "simply turning a key in a lock," say Drs. Ilg and Ames. Loose change may otherwise just disappear. "We have a kitty at home, with change for the paper boy," says Heidi. "My brother Andy, who's six, takes a lot of money from it. I threatened to tell if he didn't put it back—so he split the profits with me." Even at eleven, Heidi is not beyond temptation.

Seven is the crucial age, however, when it comes to early childhood larceny. "I see more petty thievery at age seven then at any other time, except early adolescence," Benjamin Spock noted. "At this age, the child is trying to separate himself from his parents, to rid himself of early childhood's dependence. He must develop close relationships with his peers to compensate. If he has difficulty making close friends at this stage, he may be left emotionally hungry and may turn to stealing." Or: what the child sees as a deficit of love may make him extra-hungry for possessions. This close connection, says Dr. Spock, accounts for the oddities of some of the things pilfered: a teacher's desk ornament, a best friend's special toy, things with emotional connotations.

Even with ample love, the seven-year-old, like the adolescent, is often confused by his own growing pains. He wants independence, yet fears it. He is not always certain about conforming to acceptable social behavior. Sometimes he goes on a binge of shoplifting or of "borrowing" classmate's possessions. This kind of behavior is usually temporary—especially if parents quickly respond. The normal child, say authorities, may pilfer once, or twice; if detected and forced to return the item, he seldom does it again. Parental approval is more important to him than anything else.

"When the children were between five and seven," says a Texas mother of four, "they all went through the stage of snitching candy at the grocery store. We would publicly humiliate the offending child before the store manager when we made him return the candy and apologize. I made such an emotional thing of it, and they were so humiliated, that it never happened again." A Detroit father lets the storekeeper provide the humiliation. "We've had the kids take candy from a store without paying for it. When that happens, the guilty party has to go back into the store to face the music—which means giving the candy personally back to the owner. And all the while, I hope the owner doesn't say 'that's all right,' but really gives the child a reprimand. If it happens that way, the child doesn't forget."

A West Coast seven-year-old snitched money left around the neighborhood pool during swim meets. His claim: the money was just lying around so it was all right to take it. "It was bad," says his father, "and we had a hard time breaking him of it. We talked to him and told him it was stealing. But he didn't stop until his friends got after him and his siblings let it be known that he was a fink. That did the trick."

While none of the child-development experts feels that large quantities of guilt should be induced in the young child who has picked something up for the first time—"The small thefts of the early years can usually be counted among the irregularities of normal growth," Anna W. M. Wolf wrote in *The Parent's Manual*—none thinks parents should ignore the activity either. "Show him right away that he hasn't pulled the wool over your eyes," Dr. Spock insists. "If you suspect a toy is illegitimately acquired, make him face up to it, make him make immediate restitution. Don't cooperate by pretending not to know that he snitched, or imply that in your family it's all right so long as he's not caught."

"Some guilt is downright necessary," columnist Nat Hentoff wrote recently, speaking of his own young children and a shoplifting adventure. "My wife and I made clear our total contempt for stealing and made them return the loot. They felt very guilty, and that was the end of their notion that it's a lark to snatch something that isn't yours."

It would be a mistake to allow a child to keep a stolen item, or to pay for it without requiring him to pay you back; such behavior shifts responsibility from the child to the parent. And it isn't at all necessary for the child to admit his crime for parents to take action. If you're reasonably sure goods or money were illicitly acquired—and parents should know what their children legitimately own—insisting on confession before requiring restitution just encourages the child to lie.

While a single pilfering incident with a young child need not be exaggerated in importance, it shouldn't be minimized either. It may be "just a stage," but don't pass it off as one or it may turn into more. How is the child to acquire moral values, Selma Fraiberg asks in *The Magic Years*, if parents don't react to stealing with at least the same degree of moral outrage with which they treat distasteful table manners?

A young child rarely continues stealing just to possess an item. If he continues after he is found out and reprimanded, he is more likely to be seeking peer-group approval, status, and friendship. He may steal money to buy candy to distribute, or he may simply pass out nickels and dimes; he may just announce his exploits in a bid for status. If peer groups reject the behavior, as the swimming-pool snitcher's friends did, there is likely to be a quick halt to it. If they approve, parents have a tougher job. But take heart—whatever the motivation, stealing in early childhood is generally a temporary phenomenon, one that does not lead inevitably down the garden path of juvenile delinquency.

Adolescence, with all its complexities, is a whole new ball game. Many an adult who withstood temptation as a child remembers snitching as an adolescent. "I shoplifted when I was about thirteen," says a hospital administrator, a respected member of his community, "with a group of friends, when we went to the Saturday movies. The first time I took a tape measure with a button, the second time a candy bar. I was caught with it in my pocket—and I never did it again."

But yesterday's five-cent candy bar has become today's twenty-dollar sweater, and retailers are becoming increasingly concerned over what has become a multibillion-dollar problem. The National Retail Merchants Association indicates that annual retail losses from shoplifting total $3.5 billion. That's ten million dollars a day. The average value of goods stolen in each shoplifting incident is about twenty-five dollars—hardly the kind of old-fashioned juvenile prank the neighborhood retailer might be inclined to ignore. Indeed, according to the FBI, shoplifting is the fastest growing form of larceny in the United States. Sadly, teen-agers are responsible for a large part of the problem.

Half of those arrested in one Washington, D. C., study were teen-agers. Fully two-thirds of four thousand shoplifters apprehended in New York City in one six-week period were under twenty; of these, 36 percent were under sixteen. Kids don't seem shy about admitting their activities. In 1968, 47.2 percent of one thousand Kent County, Delaware, high school students admitted shoplifting at least once. In 1973, 53 percent of the student body at Matawan Regional High School in New Jersey, 61 percent of the boys and 45 percent of the girls, said they had lifted merchandise from neighborhood stores; 81 percent fully expected to do so again.

Much attention has been paid to the radical, anti-establishment types who have made a religion of "ripping-off" the business world as a way of "beating the system." A couple of years ago newspapers reported college students brazenly wandering the aisles of a supermarket, eating lunch from the shelves. Underground newspapers urged using stolen credit cards. Thefts from college bookstores were at an all-time high. These young people who were shoplifting "on principle" now seem less evident as the political mood on the college campuses of 1974 is quiet; they never accounted for a very large share of the losses attributable to shoplifting. For the largest share we must look at ordinary kids from ordinary homes, kids not motivated by political cause or, particularly, by greed.

Lest we think these are other people's children, Robert Cain, director of the Youth Development Center of the National Council on Crime and Delinquency and former director of Delaware's Juvenile Corrections Division, stresses that "more and more shoplifters are middle-class, suburban and white." There is no correlation between family income level and shoplifting, and the young people almost always have enough money with them at the time to pay for the items they steal.

Most of these kids come from homes that are affluent or, at the very least, comfortable; except for a relative handful who need money to support a narcotics habit, they are not shoplifting for profit. They are "normal" children, not delinquents. Why do they do it?

A lot of them do it out of boredom, or for "kicks." "We hang around the Mall on Saturdays," one teen says. "Every once in a while someone suggests seeing how much we can get away with." Teen-age shoplifting, like teen-age shopping, is, for the most part, a group activity. Where town centers have been replaced as focal points by shopping centers, as in so much of American suburban sprawl, where idle teen-agers hang around stores, trouble often brews. Merchants are concerned, with reason: in St. Paul, Minnesota, a few years back, the police department reported that teen-age shoplifting in suburban shopping areas increased by 30 percent during the summer months, months when kids are out of school and more bored than usual.

Shoplifting is made all too easy, too, by today's emphasis on the wide-open look, with easily accessible goods attractively displayed in self-service stores. (With increasing losses, however, the wide-open look is giving way, in more and more stores, to more and more security: closed display cases, hidden mirrors, armed guards, electronic signals.) Advertising and its temptations are sometimes blamed too: the same ads that say buy, buy, buy, one merchant bitterly claims, bring kids into the store to steal, steal, steal.

Some teen-age shoplifting is on impulse, but much is deliberately planned, if just by a group of kids at loose ends and egging one another on. Occasionally it's more organized. School authorities have reported high school social clubs demanding stolen merchandise as an initiation fee. (Some kids resist. One study in Hawaii found that a few youngsters, eager to join the club in question but not eager to steal, purchased merchandise and claimed to have stolen it.)

Suburban communities, *The New York Times* reported in late 1972, are finding a virtual epidemic of shoplifting among the junior high school crowd. By senior high, apparently, teens find other things to do. But in early adolescence shoplifting is almost a puberty rite or, as a Connecticut teacher put it, "a rite of passage, a way that teen-agers test themselves and prove their resourcefulness and courage." Many of these kids, shoplifting because it's the "in" thing to do, give away or simply discard the merchandise they've stolen. Sometimes they keep and use it—especially the jewelry, cosmetics, and records that are favorites of teen-age shoplifters. Sometimes expensive clothing or a stereo set is teasingly displayed at home. "To be caught by your parents is almost as challenging as stealing," said one girl. "You can come up with great explanations. Convincing your parents where you got it is part of the game."

To hear authorities tell it, parents are all too willing to be convinced, unwilling to believe that their children could be involved in shoplifting. The children themselves seem to be suffering a fundamental confusion: they say they value honesty but see no relationship between shoplifting and dishonesty.

The National Retail Merchants Association confirms this assumption. Says Gordon Williams, general manager of the NRMA's Operations Division: "These youngsters simply don't realize that shoplifting is a crime. Kids who wouldn't dream of stealing money will take merchandise without a second thought." Many exhibit remarkably fuzzy thinking. "The store will never miss it," they say, totally ignorant of the actually narrow retail profit margin, or, "They figure this loss into their profits anyway."

Some youngsters won't be swayed by this logic, by the extent of store losses, or by the knowledge that shoplifting is a crime. They are the teen-agers using shoplifting as another weapon in the adolescent's perpetual war of independence, another weapon with which to attack parents; almost deliberately seeking parental attention, they are hoping to be caught. Psychiatrist Bernard S. Yudowitz calls it, "giving mother a message." And a fifteen-year-old from Colorado provides an echo: "The people I know who shoplift are plenty well off. It's one way to get attention."

Sometimes the need to get attention is so urgent that it starts in preadolescence. A letter from NRMA files:

> Dear Sirs,
> I am eleven. I read the artical [sic] on shoplifting. It was great. It's really amazing what you know about us. . . . We do what we are taught or because if we get arrested, we would like to have our parents know we exist. Once I got caught. Why? Because my mother hates me. I wanted to prove to her I was alive.
> Please send some pamphlets on why we steal. I would like to know more about myself.

Some youngsters, without the penetrating vision of this eleven-year-old, shoplift because they are caught up in the rapidly shifting emotions and philosophies of the adolescent years. There are young people who, espousing idealistic communal life and the theory that goods belong to all, yet would not steal. Others, brought up to respect private property, express their abandonment of childhood standards by shoplifting. In her definitive study, *Adolescence,* psychiatrist Irene M. Josselyn sums up the shoplifting adolescent:

He may steal in defiance of his parents' teaching over prior years because circumstances, the parents' overemphasis, or their anxiety indicates that stealing is the most effective way to rebel against his parents. He may steal because he does not differentiate between overt stealing and his father's sophisticated business dealings that are within the law because he has techniques for avoiding the law. He may steal because he wishes to perpetuate the childhood state of being given to, rather than accepting the more mature concept of the rights of others and the value of working for what he wants. He may steal, and do so clumsily, so as to be caught because he wants help. He may steal because his parents unconsciously find satisfaction in his delinquency and he unconsciously tries to gratify them. He may steal as revenge against the environment, either of his home or of his broader milieu, which has failed to meet his needs. He may steal because he has been brought up in a culture where the standards of the majority accept stealing.

One answer, it would seem, is increased parental attention. But what else can we do to forestall youthful shoplifting? We must be aware, and make our children aware, that retailers are beginning to take stringent measures. They are no longer reluctant to prosecute, and children from some very "good" families have found themselves with criminal records, records which can impede college and career plans. Parents should make a point of knowing how much money their children have and how they spend it, without snooping or disregarding every youngster's right to some privacy. Just don't close your eyes; pay attention. Don't be afraid to confront your children—like the mother who recently wrote to an advice columnist that she found several fifty-dollar bills in her son's jeans when she went to launder them, and wondered whether she had the right to ask him about them. Know your child's belongings too. "We swapped clothes," is not an acceptable explanation for an unfamiliar wardrobe, says Gordon Williams of the NRMA, unless the parents on both sides know about the swap and approve.

If an adolescent is consistently hard up for cash, he may be subject to overwhelming temptation. "Consider inflation," suggests Louise Bates Ames. "Maybe the child needs more money, a bigger allowance or ways to earn."

Set a good example yourself, say the authorities, and realize that juggling supermarket price tags, finagling on the income tax, and fixing parking tickets all contribute to an atmosphere in which it seems that there is nothing really wrong with shoplifting. The assumption that anyone is entitled to anything he can get away with, as long as he isn't caught, leads to hypocrisy, to a lesson we don't intend to teach. "My father told me never to cheat or steal," Lynn Minton writes in *The New York Times,* "and I remember my intense humiliation the day, only six years old, I received a public spanking for swiping three dimes from the windowsill where they had been left by a visiting uncle. Yet my father pushed me under the turnstile to get into the subway and got me into the movies for half price, way after I was old enough to pay full price."

A number of observers have placed the blame for increasing shoplifting squarely on the shoulders of our throw-away, disposable society, a society that revolves around a constant flow of goods, a society in which affluent youngsters have plenty of money but too little to do. It's a society, critics say, in which attitudes toward money in business and in personal life can be strikingly ambivalent. Generosity, desirable in personal life, can be a fault in business, where the profit motive reigns supreme. Most children are taught not to steal from an individual, but many families condone cheating a corporation.

Businessmen bring home office supplies; so do teachers. Hotel guests so notoriously walk off with towels, ashtrays and silverware that many hostelries are no longer placing their names on these items. The professions are not exempt. A doctor, not too long ago, stole a sphygnometer from a hospital emergency room, I was told by the hospital's administrator. He wrapped it in newspaper, tucked it under his arm, and walked out—in full view of the nurse on duty. "But you bring pencils home from the office," said the administrator's wife when he had finished the story. "That's a fringe benefit," he responded. "No," she said, "it's the same thing. But it's pennies instead of five hundred dollars."

The rise in youthful stealing, Dana L. Farnsworth, director of Harvard's health services, said in the *Wall Street Journal* a couple of years ago, reflects the morals of society. He cited a case in point: The parents of a six-year-old boy received an angry phone call from the father of their son's elementary school seatmate. The irate father complained that their son was continually stealing his son's pencils. "Understand, it's the principle of the thing," he said. "The pencils aren't important. I can get all the pencils I need from the office."

Parents must respond to continued shoplifting as they would to other youthful misdemeanors, with concern for the child and his needs rather than concern for what the neighbors will say. "What do you do when your child cheats on an exam?" a psychologist asks. "What kind of example do you set?" Parents should be aware of their own cutting corners, in daily life and in business. They should be aware of overemphasis, even if unintended, on money and possessions within the family. "Where children become superconscious of money, they begin to need it for acceptance, for self-esteem," Dr. Lee Salk observes. "Then, if they are unhappy for any reason, they may steal."

11:

Grown-Up Children

Adolescence. American parents have been so thoroughly conditioned by now that the very word strikes terror in our hearts. "Little children, little problems; big children, big problems," says one mother, with feeling. "I know we'll survive Peter's adolescence," says another, "but sometimes I'm not quite sure how."

What is an adolescent, in general, that makes him such a frightful, and frightening, creature? And, within the context of this book, how does the teen-ager, the yet-to-be adult struggling out of the cocoon, respond to money? What particular problems does he have, and does he cause his parents, with respect to money, its spending and saving, its material manifestations?

An adolescent, most simply defined, is that human being between childhood and adulthood, between puberty and maturity. As a specific, defined life stage, it is a concept new to our century, part of time and place in which biological maturity does not automatically confer adult rights and responsibilities.

It is closely linked to the affluence of a technological society that can do without the labor of young people, that has no place for them, a society that can afford to keep children in school in years when, in earlier generations, they had to be productive, a society that actually requires longer and longer periods of schooling for ever-more-sophisticated jobs.

Three major social movements made a social fact out of adolescence, psychologist David Bakan wrote in *Daedalus:* compulsory education, child labor legislation, and special legal procedures for juveniles, all of them relatively recent historical developments. In the wake of these movements, adolescence became the life stage between puberty, an identifiable biological event, and the ages specified by law for the end of education, the beginning of employment, and adult criminal procedures.

Today adolescence is longer than ever. It starts earlier, because the biological maturity which defines its onset is taking place earlier with each generation; psychoanalyst Peter Blos has declared that puberty begins four months earlier with each decade. One wonders where that will leave us eventually—perhaps with adolescents in the cradle—but at the moment the erratic behavior that seems to characterize adolescence, at least partly attributable to the confusing hormonal changes that accompany puberty, are noticeable in some youngsters, especially girls, as early as nine or ten. Girls do mature earlier, and become adolescents, at least as physically defined, about two years earlier than their male schoolmates.

And adolescence lasts longer now. With more and more young people going to school longer and longer, thus delaying the assumption of adult responsibility which characterizes the end of adolescence (blue-collar workers who take jobs at the end of high school, often marrying early too, are adults years before their middle-class contemporaries who go on to college and graduate school), the upper limits of adolescence are constantly being pushed outward.

Whatever the specific brackets—and, of course, they vary as

much as behavior does in individual youngsters—early adolescence is characterized almost universally by the first stirrings of independence, a shaking loose of parental control. But, at least at first, it's very much a back-and-forth motion: defy parents one moment, reach for their support the next. Psychiatrist Irene M. Josselyn defines this period as a time of "chaos, contradictory behavior, and unpredictable responses." As a parent puts it: "Joanie is agreeable one moment, all sugar and spice, and the next she dissolves in tears for no reason that I can see." And another: "Independence is all he talks about—'I'm not a child anymore' is the constant refrain—but nonetheless he seems to turn to us for guidance almost as much, sometimes more often, than before."

Adolescent attitudes toward money reflect this ambivalence. At every age money, because it has so much symbolic value, is an easily grasped vehicle for emotional expression. In adolescence it becomes a symbol for all kinds of intergenerational conflict. It is a weapon used by both sides in the battle, as children alternately struggle for independence and seek support, and parents waver between pushing them out of the nest and retaining control.

As part of his rebellion against his family, part of the healthy assertion of individuality that marks growing up, the teen-ager may reject family patterns of thrift and expenditure just as he, usually temporarily, rejects other parental behavior. Thus he may become loudly critical of his parents' economic struggles or of their financial successes. "We don't seem to have done anything right," says one father.

In his own spending, the adolescent is often totally inconsistent. "He may be alternately tightfisted and wildly spendthrift," Frances Lomas Feldman writes in *The Family in a Money World.* He resents it if his parents let him spend freely, particularly if he makes a poor purchase. But he insists on buying what pleases him and often spends his money defiantly.

What pleases him, at this stage, is often what pleases the crowd. Securing the approval of friends becomes far more important in early adolescence, at least on the surface, than maintaining the approval of parents. Recent reassuring studies have shown that teen-agers do, contrary to appearances, rely on parents in important matters: decisions about college, about careers. But in the superficial matters, the clothes they wear, the length of their hair, the records they have to own and must incessantly play—issues that aren't really issues but can be very divisive—peer-group approval is all-important. Conforming to the constantly shifting currents of the youth culture requires money. Being able to purchase the correct uniform is of crucial importance. Social status, in adolescent eyes, can rise or fall on the issue of conformity in possessions.

"Clothes were all that counted in my high school," a young woman recalls bitterly. "If you wore the same thing to school twice in one month, you were dead socially. I didn't have the kind of money, or the kind of wardrobe, that permitted me to keep up, and I was never one of the crowd." Thirty-one now, the memory is vivid.

Today's fashions may seem less demanding—patched and embroidered jeans are not costly to maintain—but teens still feel the need to conform. In many suburbs, the automobile is the ultimate teen-age possession. The youngster, especially the boy, who has a car is socially supreme; the one who does not is at the low end of the social totem pole. The auto fetish, if such it is, has been traditional for decades, ever since the automobile began to symbolize power and freedom. But now that so many teens have cars (adequate student parking facilities are a major problem at many suburban high schools) the auto is being replaced as a status symbol by motorcycles, surfboards, scuba equipment, gliders, and snowmobiles. How is a parent to cope with such demands?

"That's easy; I just say no," says one father bluntly. But another asks, "Isn't it important for them to have what their friends do?" And, queries a third, "If they earn the money themselves, do I have any right to tell them how to spend it?"

There's no simple answer to these legitimate questions. Few parents feel comfortable always saying "no," especially if the family can afford the request. It *is* important for children, of all ages, to fit in with their friends. But it is equally important to retain some perspective. If some desired extravagance is way out of line with the family's standard of living, or with parental values, it is certainly not amiss for a parent to say so. "A snowmobile? I should say not," is one way to close a discussion. Or, if the child is simply too young, say so. "We'll talk about a motorcycle when you're seventeen, not before." It doesn't really matter who earned the money; parents have a right—and an obligation—to impose standards.

Despite constant publicity about extravagant teen-agers, most youngsters seem to have their heads firmly attached to their shoulders. "My parents give me five dollars a week," says one tenth grader. "That covers lunches, and I baby-sit for extras." "I earn as much as I can," says a high school senior in an upper-middle-class community. "I don't want to keep taking money from my parents."

Youngsters brought up to view money as a practical tool, neither overly casually nor with undue respect, by parents with whom they've had reasonably good interaction through the childhood years, seldom go off the deep end in adolescence. Those with emotional problems, however, may, just like adults, reveal their inner turmoil in the way they handle money. In an article entitled "Money: An Index to Personal Problems in Adolescents" in the August 1963 issue of *Marriage and Family Living,* Frances Lomas Feldman of the University of Southern California points to danger signals displayed by certain consistent patterns of behavior toward money. There is the teen who is constantly the center of an after-school candy store crowd, buying friendships he cannot otherwise establish. There is the youngster who continually borrows, both money and tangible items, from everyone in sight, and who becomes angry when he is denied what he unconsciously views as affection. There is the hoarder, for whom money "is tangible and incontrovertible evidence that he is strong; it is through money that he gains his esteem." There is the adolescent who must know the price of every item newly acquired by a classmate—and who then competitively rushes out to purchase something at least as good. All of these individuals "have shifted to financial symbols the values of affection and security normally instilled in childhood."

Adolescent attitudes toward money stem from early experiences, the areas we have been exploring throughout this book. But adolescence is a special time of its own, a vulnerable time in which defenses are often temporarily erected against a threatening world. Thus, while consistently irrational behavior with money may suggest emotional problems, we must remember that adolescents are typically inconsistent, irrational one moment, cooly logical the next. Don't look for trouble by reading neurotic symptoms into normal teen-age behavior. Try, hard as it may be, to maintain a balance, to offer your teen-ager some freedom to spend and to make mistakes, within firm family standards.

Right now it's stylish among the younger set to disdain possessions—but the disdain seems very unreal to many parents, a pure example of adolescent illogic. "Kids are anti-materialistic after they have everything," says a mother whose six children, now between fourteen and twenty-five, have given her ample opportunity to observe. "They go off to college scoffing at money—and with their cars loaded with stereos, guitars, typewriters, etc., etc., etc." Says E. B. Weiss of Doyle Dane Bernback: "They have talked a much better game of deploring conspicuous consumption than they play."

The definition of materialism seems to vary with the generations. "They think we're materialistic if we save money, but they're not if they spend it. You have to be fourteen to follow the logic," says one mother. "There are bitter accusations and recriminations between adults and young people in regard to the value of money," Gisela Konopka, professor of social work at the University of Minnesota, wrote in *The Function of Rebellion—Is Youth Creating New Family Values?*, a report of the Child Study Association of America's 1968 conference. "Many adults feel that the young, having grown up with no experience in a world of deprivation, take money for granted and do not understand the sacrifices the parents have made. To the young, the older generation, with its concern with money, seems like a very materialistic one."

Young people may not be materialistic, by their own definition, but they sure do like the things that money can buy. Their priorities are sometimes interesting. *The New York Times* pointed to one college senior who has "a $2,850 MGB sports car, $20 cowboy boots and one pair of now-patched dungarees which he bought last summer for $7 and now wears 'practically every day.' "

Perhaps youngsters reared in an era of affluence literally don't understand the concept of saving for a rainy day; perhaps it looks to them like an overpreoccupation with money. If so, some education is in order. We must somehow convey to this generation that affluence is not an ordained state of affairs, that there is such a thing as an unpredictable future. They might actually appreciate the knowledge. Affluence was cited as a major personal problem by a majority of youngsters recently surveyed by the Rand Youth Poll. Too much money, too many material things bestowed by parents, "erodes motivation, detracts from responsibility, makes it difficult for them to function," says Lester Rand. "Young people find it difficult to live with."

So do their parents. Many of today's middle generation are uncomfortably caught in a dilemma. They are glad to be able to give their children a worry-free life, to provide the security they themselves might not have known. "I was working at nine, delivering rolls for a local bakery," one New York father says. "My kids won't have to do that." Yet the same parents feel, in a way, that today's kids have it too easy, that, as Lester Rand says, it isn't doing them a favor to give them too much. "He can't possibly appreciate a car as much if I buy it for him as if he earns it himself," a Depression-reared parent insists. "We sure appreciated every last thing we were able to get to make life easier, because we worked for it; nobody handed us anything on a silver platter."

But we can't reverse the clock. We can't artificially create a sense of purpose, of the need for hard work that outside economic conditions so skillfully create. Artificial deprivation only breeds resentment. "I know my parents can afford to buy me a car," a high school student says, "but they insist I'll learn something by earning the money for it. That doesn't make any sense. They're just being selfish." Parents may try to sustain the virtues of an economically difficult time, the qualities of austerity and self-help, in their children, August Heckscher wrote in *The Nation's Children*, but "they find this to be an almost impossible task. The children are of their own time; its standards and tendencies speak to them compellingly." Somehow we must attempt to steer a middle course, to bring up kids who can handle affluence, a younger generation that doesn't expect to be handed the world on the proverbial silver platter.

"Why fix something, the kids say. Just buy a new car if the old one needs repairs. It's frivolous to repair things in the house. If we say it costs too much to just buy a new whatever-it-is, if it would be wasteful to throw something away that can be fixed—like a car!" this father says incredulously, "they say we're being materialistic." But a lot of this kind of talk is just that—talk. Youngsters taught to be resourceful, to think first of fixing something, then if necessary of replacement, are likely to revert to that pattern after the stormy rebellion of adolescence, when fixing things, conserving, may serve as another example of adult stodginess.

Despite their self-attributed antimaterialism, despite their idealism (if you take material comfort for granted, you can afford to be idealistic, says one perhaps-cynical observer), kids are self-interested too. Teens are enormously interested in cleaning up the environment and curbing pollution; 98.3 percent promise to curb littering, *Seventeen* magazine found in a 1973 survey. But only one in five of this same altruistic group would be willing to do without an automobile.

Parents, of course, can be as inconsistent as their offspring. Money becomes a powerful tool in the struggle for independence, a tool wielded by both sides. Some parents, unconsciously competing with their children, deny them funds in an effort to retain control. Some feel a perfectly normal desire to postpone their own advancing age—but implement that desire by keeping their children dependent. Others encourage self-sufficiency. "I feel like a real cheapskate," the mother of a sixteen-year-old college freshman says, "but she used our telephone credit card to make a long-distance call and I sent her the bill. She can pay for it out of her allowance." Others gladly accept collect calls from long-since-grown children.

Youngsters, particularly in late adolescence, can earn more and more of their own keep. Where one eighteen-year-old can be self-supporting right out of high school, his college-bound contemporary can still earn enough part-time to avoid total psychological dependence on his family. Sometimes a high school student can be more independent in this regard than a college student. "I earned money all through high school as a short-order cook," says one such college freshman, "and never asked my parents for anything. I bought my own stereo and financed my own trip to Europe last summer. Now I'm at college and too busy this first year to work. It just kills me to know that every time I buy a beer my parents are paying for it."

Others expect indefinite support. "I had one semester at college and hated it," said a nineteen-year-old dropout, an American, who was cleaning a bathroom on an Israeli kibbutz. "All anyone was interested in was cars and dates. They were all completely dependent on momma's and poppa's pocketbook. They bitched about them but wouldn't dream of cutting loose and being on their own." This girl did cut loose, all the way. Other dropouts, dozens of them, can be found on the fringes of almost any college town; some are still supported by parents faithfully sending room, board, and tuition money to youngsters enjoying every aspect of college life except, unbeknownst to their parents, classes.

Today's adolescents, brought up in a time and place in which they know no deprivation, expect to enjoy the good things in life as a birthright—whether they or their parents actually pay the bills. Sometimes the fine distinction of who pays is blurred. One young man told an interviewer he was financially independent, then admitted that his father bought the car he drives and pays for its insurance, that he accepts cash birthday and Christmas gifts from his parents, and that he even put last summer's plane fare to Europe on his father's credit card. Independent?

This generation expects to enjoy the fruits of their own labor. "I am very much bothered," says a Denver parent, "by teens who feel, 'If I get a job I can buy a car,' without a thought for the total family, the other needs of the family. This is not financial responsibility." But it stems from growing up in families where there is little actual need, where the contributions of children are neither needed nor of much use. "Much of the hedonistic outlook of our younger generation," Bruno Bettelheim wrote in *Children of the Dream*, "has its roots in this fact: the essentials of life seem to come without exertion.... The middle-class child depends on his parents for both the essentials and extras, but has no clear idea of what it takes to provide the essentials. Hence those children whom all the extras do not seem to satisfy, because without a clear feeling for the essentials, they really are not enough." "They seem to take everything for granted," a father complains; "nothing that we do is ever enough."

This generation is the despair of their college placement officers, Caroline Bird wrote about the class of 1973 in *New York Magazine*. "Although almost all the record 981,000 who received bachelor's or first professional degrees this year have earned at least some money at some time in their lives, and many have been trained for business or a profession, most of them are appallingly uninformed about how 'adults' earn the money that supported them through college." According to Melvin Helitzer, who has spent his business career selling to young people, "Kids simply don't understand the value of money. There is complete bewilderment in their twenties over things they should have known in their teens—all because we keep postponing adulthood." This endless willingness to take, it should be noted, is typical only of young people from affluent backgrounds. "Anyone who has grown up in poverty or on the edge," says Ellen Manser of the Family Service Association of America, "is dying to get out, and is convinced that the only way out of it is through work. The affluent kids of the suburbs feel it's family responsibility to put no strings on anything, to just keep on giving."

Because middle-class young people have always had so much, they feel free to reject it—knowing that it will be there waiting for them should they decide to return. The adolescent who opts out of working, the teen who sneers at material possessions, the Vassar graduate who goes to work as a cowgirl—they know in their bones, though they may not articulate the feeling, that if and when they decide to drop back in, they will be welcomed. They feel secure.

At the same time, much of today's younger generation is uninterested in working for money alone. Idealistic, they are dedicated to solving the world's problems, uninterested in conventional business careers, careers that typify traditional economic and material values. This idealism has always been typical of young people, out to reform the world before they adapt to it. But today's disenchantment with the world of work is, for the first time, characteristic of much of the adult population as well, and of blue-collar workers as well as white. As jobs become more fragmented, there is less visible result, and far less reward available on the job or from the job. In traditional societies work is part of life, inseparable from what you are, Yale psychologist Kenneth Keniston observes. "For most Americans, in contrast, 'work' has vaguely unpleasant connotations. . . . The goal of work is to earn the money necessary for 'living' when one is not working. . . . Implicitly, work is seen as a necessary instrumental evil without inherent meaning." If this is so, if we convey to our children that work isn't much fun, is only peripheral to life, it's easy to see why they are disinterested. "Our younger son, in complete contrast to his brother, was completely turned off in high school, uninterested in earning the grades that would get him into college," says a social worker. "He said, when we tried to convince him that schooling is important, 'So what's so great about what you and

Dad do? You both have master's degrees and you come home every night and complain. Why should I do all this work and wind up hating life, as you seem to do, be dead and have nothing to show for it?' We had always said that home was where you let it all hang out but we decided to start talking about the joys of our work and keep the frustrations quiet for a while."

It is hazardous, of course, to characterize the "younger generation"—not only because, like any generation, it is made up of individuals rather than a mass of undifferentiated humanity but because it changes with great rapidity. The impact of college kids was so pervasive during the Vietnam years, according to Melvin Helitzer, "that if we could sell them products we knew it would filter down to their younger brothers and sisters as well as influencing their parents; college kids were pace-setters. Within sixty days of the American pullout from Vietnam and within two or three months of the end of the draft, the whole mood of the country changed. With the elimination of fear, of the needle stuck in a vital part of them, there were no more protests and almost a return to the beat generation, an attitude of 'leave me alone.' " Sociologist Mathew Greenwald confirms this observation: "There's been a big change in the last year; young people are less involved outwardly, more self-involved, introspective."

This attitude has implications for career choice too. In the 1960s college students turned away from business occupations in droves, rejecting the traditional Puritan work ethic. Now student interest in business careers is on the upswing. Only 3 percent of those surveyed by Gallup in 1962 favored a business executive's career; in 1973 the figure was 9 percent. And the American Council on Education found 17.1 percent of incoming freshmen in September 1972 heading for probable business careers. But motivation has changed. "If making a lot of money ever was the chief motivation for studying business," *The New York Times* reports, "it no longer is ... instead, finding interesting work and its geographical locations are their first concerns."

Disenchantment with the world of work is being channeled into insistence that work must be rewarding. "Work used to be something you got paid for," sociologist Mathew Greenwald observes, "now it's also something which has to be fulfilling, significant. As expectations become different, it's harder to be satisfied." Interestingly, working-class young people, affected by social change, are moving closer and closer to the attitudes of college students. A massive, in-depth study by Daniel Yankelovich, released in May 1974, indicates that blue-collar young are more and more espousing the attitudes that marked college youth of five years ago—and becoming increasingly dissatisfied and frustrated at a sense of unfulfillment. But, Yankelovich reported, according to *The New York Times*, "as workers move closely to what college students were, the students of today are predisposed to reconcile themselves to society, feel less alienation and hope they will be able to function constructively within it."

There have been other recent changes in the work ethic. In 1970, in the first of a series of studies on *Finance-Related Attitudes of Youth*, the Institute of Life Insurance reported that four out of five of the fourteen- to twenty-five-year-olds surveyed felt that a person should be responsible for taking care of himself. Those already out of school felt the need and desire to be self-sufficient even more strongly than did the younger group. "I'm too old to be taking from my parents," a twenty-year-old-college girl insists.

In sharp contrast, the 1972 follow-up study found that 28 percent (up from 18 percent in 1970) felt that "it's all right to rely on others (e.g., government, family) for financial aid." The shift is especially significant among that older group, on the job, often married and with children, who traditionally have expected to be on their own. "This change of view may be the result of two contemporary factors," the report notes, "the recent financial hardships many people have faced through unemployment and inflation, and a weakening of values associated with the Protestant Ethic, a value system which stresses hard work, individualism and self-reliance." "My grandmother won't accept Medicare," sociologist Greenwald says, "but there are kids in communes who sue their parents so that they can become emancipated minors eligible to receive welfare." College students gladly accept food stamps. Handouts are expected, and acceptable.

As attitudes toward work change, as value systems shift, more and more young people are exploring communes, collectives, and varying alternate life-styles. In 1965 there were approximately one hundred communes in the United States; by 1971 there were at least three thousand. It's hard to be precise because they form and dissolve with ease. But most, contrary to popular opinion, are located in urban areas. Some are strictly rent-sharing arrangements—much as college students and young career people have done for generations; others are more idealistic, life-and-philosophy-sharing communes, formed by young people consciously rejecting what they see as overmaterialism in society at large. These emphasize common property, thus effectively deterring membership among those who care a great deal for personal possessions—the young man with a prized stereo set, for example, loathe to have it mangled by many hands. For most, however, the communal way of life is a waystation, a temporary stage.

The commune movement, still, attracts no more than a small minority of young people. Although as many as one in four surveyed by the Institute of Life Insurance in 1972 think they may give it a try, most regard it as a temporary phase and expect to choose a more traditional family arrangement when it comes to permanent choice. In fact, when it comes to long-range life-style preference, 32 percent of the young men surveyed would choose to be successful executives or professionals, living with wives and children in good areas. Another 20 percent expect to be average family men, with routine jobs, time for family and outside interests. Only 13 percent expected to be free of obligations, living where and with whom they pleased.

Perhaps the sharpest possible contrast in the shadowy portrait of young people lies between the eagerly anticipated (by

advertisers) bridal market on the one hand, and the postponement of adult responsibilities by a small, but growing and
articulate, group on the other. *Seventeen* magazine has pages
chock-full of ads for china and silver, furniture and appliances;
95.2 percent of its teen-age readers, despite their growing interest in careers, still plan to marry and to marry fairly young.
Despite changing life-styles, despite their (theoretical?) antimaterialism, these young American women look ahead eagerly
to marriage, to a vine-covered cottage filled with appliances.
"When I get married I'll take all my things from my mother's
house," says a seventeen-year-old midwesterner, "and we'll
buy a dishwasher and a washing machine right away."

Parents can usually accept this outlook, although some may
deplore the eager desire for possessions. What's harder to accept, for virtually every parent, is delayed adolescence. There
have always been some young people reluctant to settle down;
today there are enough to make a noticeable impact on society
as a whole. It's a phenomenon that begins with upper-middle-
class affluent youth, young people whose families can afford
their dalliance, much as adolescence first became a recognized
life-stage among the well-to-do. It's a phenomenon that mani-
fests itself as endless schooling, interrupted by or followed by
travel, then, perhaps, graduate school and/or a period of volunteer work until, suddenly, Junior is twenty-eight and still
not self-supporting. "I want to bum around the world for a few
years," a college dropout told me. "I don't know what will be in
a few years. I can always go back to school." "Unusually large
numbers of those who entered the class as freshmen have
dropped out," Caroline Bird wrote about the class of 1973,
"and a lot of those who stuck it out felt they urgently needed a
spell of R&R."

The phenomenon has become common enough—as more
parents, commiserating with each other about these children
they cannot understand, discover that they are not alone—so
that behavioral scientists are giving it a name. "Millions of
young people today are neither psychological adolescents nor

sociological adults," psychologist Kenneth Keniston wrote in *Youth and Dissent*. He calls "these young men and women of college- and graduate-school age who can't seem to 'settle down' the way their parents did, who refuse to consider themselves adult," participants in a new phase of life, one Keniston terms Youth. Sociologists Mathew Greenwald and Carl Danziger call it Transadulthood.

In a study sponsored by the Institute of Life Insurance, Danziger and Greenwald, then both at Rutgers, wrote: "It is now becoming apparent that society is recognizing another stage in the process of becoming grownup. This can best be called transadulthood, which extends from entrance to college, or the end of adolescence, to an indefinite point in the late twenties or early thirties. It is a period of experimenting with different life-styles, of searching for career orientation, and for testing educational goals. It is often a time in which responsibilities are minimized and personal freedom is maximized. The desire to keep options open, to be constantly flexible and prepared for change, is characteristic of the transadult."

This may be an elaborate way of defining what some parents call laziness. Says one father: "Too many kids have their way paid all the way through college and then need two years on the road or in Europe to 'find themselves.'" Says another: "They're delighted to postpone responsibility. And we're all envious of their freedom." But Greenwald and Danziger see the stage as a legitimate portion of the life cycle, albeit one that is not yet officially sanctioned (as adolescence was not universally recognized as a developmental stage before the early twentieth century). "I think work as part of life is going to contract," Mathew Greenwald told me, "with five recognizable stages in life, only one of which entails work: childhood, adolescence, transadulthood, work, and retirement."

Parents, reared in the work ethic, find this difficult to understand, or to appreciate. "My twenty-three-year-old brother, a history major, worked for a year with retarded youngsters, then traveled, still doesn't know what he wants to do," Mathew

Greenwald says, drawing on an example close to home. "My parents are uptight; they expect job and marriage from a twenty-three-year-old."

As college becomes a necessity instead of a luxury, something an affluent society can provide for more of its children; as the women's movement convinces more young women that they needn't marry early just because it's the thing to do, or out of a fear that it's early or never; as alternate life-styles become more acceptable; as more couples live together openly, at least temporarily, without benefit of clergy, more young adults will defer commitment to career and to marriage, defer the assumption of adult responsibilities, be characterized as trans-adults or, in Keniston's term, youth.

Parents are frequently bewildered, "uptight," at this behavior. A recent *McCall's* article by Norman Lobsenz speaks of the "generational squeeze," in which middle-aged adults are being caught between the anticipated needs of elderly parents and the unexpected dependencies of their grown children. "More and more teen-agers now take a year or more off between high school and college or during college. They put off taking a serious job or settling into a career to 'find themselves'—and thus postpone the time when they can be self-supporting." It's undeniably difficult for parents. "Paul bummed around for four years after college," one such mother told me. "We thought he would never settle down. Now he's home again and working and it begins to look as if he'll make it. We're glad, of course—but it isn't easy having him living at home again when we thought he'd be on his own by now."

Parents may have to recognize, along with the social scientists, that this is a new phase of life, one that does not imply permanent disaster. "I think these young adults are still concerned about success in the work world," says Greenwald, "but there's an ambivalence. They're not sure they can get exactly the kind of fulfilling job they want, make a success of it; at the same time they're fearful of getting into a rut. This leads to trying alternatives. But parents needn't panic. Virtually all go back to the values they're brought up with. After the experience, a beneficial one, of traveling, trying a commune, working for the post office, they will come back to standard values, values of which their parents approve. They won't be bums," Greenwald insists, "and they will be better people, more satisfied with their jobs and their marriages when they do make a commitment, more likely to be stable in both."

12:

Talking Things Over

Communication, according to the *Random House Dictionary of the English Language,* is the act or process of communicating, "the imparting or interchange of thoughts, opinions, or information by speech, writing, or signs." Simple enough. And yet . . .

Problems in communication are the single most frequent area of marital conflict in families above the poverty level; relationships with children run second. Fully 44 percent of all couples with one problem also report the other, according to a study by the Family Service Association of America. Combined with the testimony of scores of parents and children, it might seem that intergenerational conflict within the family, an inability to communicate, runs rampant throughout America.

"I see it all the time," says a Youth Guidance Council worker in a small New England town, speaking of youngsters who have been in minor trouble with the law. "If the lines of communication are open between parent and child the problem can almost solve itself. If they're not open we get the same offense repeated over and over again." In ordinary families as well, with ordinary problems, where there is no run-in with legal authority and no thought of need for professional counseling, lines of communication often seem to diverge as children reach adolescence, as if two different languages are being spoken.

To some extent this is only natural, as adolescents, preoccupied with their own concerns, are growing up into a world of their own making while their parents remain preoccupied with the world of the present. Too much divergence, of course, and a temporary rift between mercurial adolescents and set-in-their-ways parents may become permanent, communication may cease altogether. Yet thousands of families, quietly going their own way, have no problems with communication, no break in rapport, no stereotypical impenetrable barrier between parents and their adolescent children. Just how much of a generation gap is there?

A lot may depend on the eye of the beholder. When *Scholastic Magazine*'s National Institute of Student Opinion queried students in the 1971–72 school year, 32 percent said there was no gap at all in their families, 51 percent said there was a gap, but not a large one, and only 16 percent admitted to a gulf between the generations. Many say there is a gap . . . but not in their own families.

Where there is a gap it is often very much issue-related. Today's different values, tastes and morals—and parental failure to understand them—are at the root of the conflict.

The issue may, at times, be money. Adolescent attitudes sometimes seem composed of one part casual acceptance of support as their due, while they plan their ideal life, and one part philosophical rejection of everything the older generation represents, especially material success. "My father does nothing but earn money. I know it's supposed to be for us, but he's so tired at night that I can't even get his attention. That's no way to live." Some young people, in their idealism, repudiate all materialism; others become superconscious of money and incredibly materialistic. Sometimes the same exuberant youngster will veer from one extreme to the other.

Nonetheless, most parents find the communication gap, if they have one, a temporary, if annoying, pushing away of parents by children struggling to grow up. But during this trying period many, on both sides of the generational fence, cry out for attention. "They never stay at home once they get to be teen-agers," a parent complains. "How can we talk to them if they're not here?" A young man from a different family, not quite sure why his parents want him to stay home evenings, might have an answer. "They don't talk to me anyway," he shrugs. "I stay home and then they watch television, or sit and read. I guess they just want to know I'm there."

Ellen Manser of the Family Service Association of America offers some guidelines for keeping the intergenerational lines of communication open. First and foremost, she says, try not to reminisce. "My kids made a joke about it with my husband, who grew up in Oregon and actually walked two miles to school through snowdrifts. 'Two miles through two feet of snow carrying two pounds of books,' was chanted by the boys, in unison, when we showed any signs of reminiscing. The sense of humor saved us." It's very difficult for parents to feel confident about all the differences today, Mrs. Manser readily concedes, but telling kids about "in my day" doesn't help at all. They just begin to feel that it's impossible to make their parents understand, and they don't talk at all. And that's the second point: listen, to whatever your children have to say. "Don't mumble a response when he talks about movies or rock groups and wait for the golden moments that never come when you can have a 'worthwhile' conversation." Pay attention, when your children talk about anything at all, and communication can be sustained. The third point: patience. They do grow out of it. They do, given time, become people with whom you can communicate on an adult level. They do, in fact, become adults.

But communication refers to far more than the generation gap. It also concerns the ways in which family decisions are made, whether the family is autocratic or democratic. And it relates to the sharing of specific, often economic, information.

One of the reasons many families never lose the ability to communicate, on some level, even with adolescent children, is the increasing democratization of the American family, a family in which children, almost from birth, are expected to be heard as well as seen. The family council as a formal institution may not be commonplace but give-and-take, the input of ideas from every member of the family, is more and more expected as a matter of course. Some observers are upset by this sociologically well-documented trend, thinking it undermines parental authority; most think, properly handled, it is positive. After all, whether Junior puts in his two cents with respect to what he wants for dinner, what kind of car the family should buy, or where to go on vacation, he becomes accustomed, at an early age, to participating, to communicating his ideas, to thinking them through so that he can defend them. And parents, on the whole, listen, take the suggestions seriously and explain, when necessary, why they can't or won't be accepted.

This willingness to listen and to discuss need not imply an abdication of parental responsibility. "Where feasible, we do what the kids want to do," one father says, "but if it's something on which we can make the best decision, if there clearly is a 'best' decision, then we just do." Family discussions actually induce greater conformity, sociologist George Psathas observes, since the child, after discussion, often shares the opinion of his parents. And Reuben Hill of the University of Minnesota, in his study of family life over three generations, found that shared decision-making results in stronger families.

This form of communication, the sharing of ideas, participation in decision-making, is usually unplanned, spontaneous. It is simply part of the fabric of life—and an excellent learning tool, as children learn from a very early age why some items can be purchased and others not, some activities undertaken and others not.

Part of this understanding comes from learning what things

cost—another aspect of parent-child communication. While some parents deliberately withhold knowledge of any and all expenditures from their children, others feel, often strongly, that kids can't learn to manage money solely through buying candy bars; they must have some realistic idea of how larger sums are spent before they have larger sums to manage. This need not mean explaining the mortgage—"the fact that you owe thirty thousand dollars on a mortgage on your house is totally incomprehensible to the small child," says Louise Bates Ames—but it can involve sharing, gradually, information about day-to-day living costs—food, clothing, vacations—the things, says Dr. Ames, that directly concern the child.

The most important thing to share with children, especially with preadolescents, is a sense of priorities, of making choices. Where to stay on vacation is one such choice, what kind of coat to buy is another. The New York nine-year-old who wants a rug and a comfortable chair for her room is allowed to choose which one she wants most for this year's birthday present; both at once, she is told, are too costly. "We don't talk about salary," says a Denver aerospace engineer, father of an eight-year-old and a five-and-a-half-year-old, "but we do discuss such things as not getting so much for Christmas and getting a trampoline later, or waiting to get the couch upholstered because of job uncertainty."

All children, those of superaffluent parents as well as those in families with job uncertainty, should understand that money is a finite commodity, that priorities must be established. "Children should have a general idea of the limitations of family income," a psychologist insists. "If you imply that you can't afford anything or that you can afford everything, it denies them a real ability to deal with the world."

Today, of course, inflation is forcing even the affluent to make choices. But even where funds aren't greatly limited, in upper-upper income families, it's wise to teach kids to choose, to set priorities, to slowly absorb the concept of what money, in substantial amounts, can do. Children's ability to comprehend large figures, after all, to relate value to money, is totally unconnected with the wealth of the family. And, in wealthy families as in the prosaic middle class, every child's understanding is aided by reducing large figures to manageable components. If, for example, a summer camp charges $60 for a season of horseback riding, as an optional extra, you might point out to a curious youngster that that pays for two hours a week for eight weeks, or sixteen hours for $60, or $3.75 a lesson. Three dollars and seventy-five cents is a sum most nine-year-olds can grasp; $60 is not.

Children in the primary grades, overawed by large amounts, tend to take their parents' long-range financial planning—the college bank account, for example—for granted, if they give it a thought. Many teen-agers, planning higher education, are delighted with parental and grandparental help. But adolescents, cantankerous as they can be, often have independent ideas. "We don't dare tell Sheila that we have a savings account designed for her college education," the mother of a strong-willed red-haired sixteen-year-old says. "She'd insist that she has no intention of going to college and hassle us unmercifully to give her the money so she could travel. Since we have no intention of doing any such thing, we just don't mention it." With relatives who do insist on recognition, the child could simply be told that the gift has strings attached; it goes toward education unless and until it is clear to everyone, at some far future date, that their education is complete.

A similar problem exists when the nest egg is government bonds or corporate shares, whether it be a large portfolio in an affluent family or a few shares acquired by scrimping and saving. Little is gained by telling the children too much too soon. One well-to-do Westchester pediatrician plans to inform his sons of their holdings before they enter college. Meanwhile, his fourth grader, excited by a social studies lesson on the stock market, determined to buy himself one share of stock. He raked leaves and did every garden chore he could find until he earned enough—never dreaming that he already owned a considerable portfolio.

Another nuts-and-bolts aspect of specific communication,

one often overlooked, is family discussion of wills and guardians. Seldom discussed even with grown children, these matters are almost never raised with little ones. But, surprisingly often, young children, becoming aware that all living things die and sensing that their total security derives from their parents, want to know what will happen to them when their parents die. A frequent off-the-cuff response by a flustered parent is: "Oh, that won't happen until you're all grown up and a mommy, or daddy, yourself. Don't think about it now." This may be so, in most cases, but it doesn't get at the root of the child's concern; he really does want to know what will happen to *him*.

No matter how small you think your estate will be, you should have a will. It's the only way to be sure that whatever money you have is distributed according to your wishes and not dissipated by legal costs involved in determining who gets what. In that will you should have named a guardian for your minor children, giving the choice great thought. The ideal person to raise your children, should necessity demand, is not necessarily the closest relative available, not unless his ideas and values are those you want your children to have.

Once you have made a will and, carefully, selected a guardian, you can respond to your youngster's inevitable question with: "Parents usually live a long long time, until after their children are all grown up and have children of their own. But, if anything did happen to us, Aunt Lil and Uncle Dan will take care of you." At this age, financial details are unnecessary.

With very much older children, if they will inherit substantial amounts, preparation might be in order—not only basic consumer training, if you will, but advanced training to deal with large sums. You will have named a guardian to physically care for a minor child, of course, and executors to safeguard the estate. But young people themselves can plan ahead if they know what to expect. Wisely worded wills, these days, often stagger an inheritance so that much of it is retained in trust until the recipient is more than mature. Rather than turn an entire estate over to a child upon his eighteenth or even his twenty-first birthday, more and more lawyers recommend distribution over a period of years: one-third at twenty-one, for example, one-third at thirty, and the remainder at thirty-five or even forty. By then, your training in money management will surely have taken hold. Meanwhile, sharing this kind of information, letting the kids know what's in store, even in broad outline, should avoid at least one kind of dream-world confusion: the twenty-year-old who, it was reported to me, asked her father if she would get her inheritance promptly on her twenty-first birthday. When he, a healthy man in his mid-forties, expressed shocked bewilderment, and asked what on earth she was talking about, she responded, in all innocence: "But everyone gets an inheritance at twenty-one."

College-bound youngsters, some economists claim, often learn far less of the real dollar-and-cents world than those whose education ends with high school. Locked in to academic, college-entrance courses, they seldom get a taste of the home economics, business, and consumer education classes that provide a basis for knowledgeable consumer behavior. It's up to parents, then, to make a point of conveying the major financial facts of life before their seventeen- and eighteen-year-olds leave the nest. These youngsters should, over the high school years, have assumed some responsibility for their own clothes purchases. They should know what college costs, what it takes to live away from home, to pay for meals and a place to sleep and, looking ahead, have an idea of the input and outgo of the world beyond school.

For a great many young people, and their parents, college brings a rude financial awakening. College costs have jumped by more than a third in the past four years, and very few youngsters are not helping to meet the bills. Even parents with combined incomes of $40,000 a year frequently need their help, especially if more than one child is in school at the same time. Average student expenditures for the 1974–1975 school year, reported in *The New York Times,* run to $4,039 at a private residential college (the Ivy League is still more), $2,400 at a public live-in college. Commuting students pay less, but not so much less as might be thought; in a four-year private college the tab is $3,683 and in a public institution it is $2,085.

A survey by the New York State Education Department shows that 88 percent of the students in private colleges and 82 percent of those at state universities (in New York) hold summer jobs to help defray college costs; almost one-quarter of all students work all year round. The latest wrinkle—a result of the legal age being lowered to eighteen—is that some parents have financially disowned their children, at least in terms of income taxes and college applications. "If he's old enough to vote, he's on his own," says one such parent. "Maybe he can get financial help from school as an individual; with my salary we're too rich for help and too poor to afford college." Whether parents help or not—and most still do—college-bound youngsters learn, willy-nilly, like it or not, what education costs. But they still may not know, and may never know, parental income.

By far the most sensitive topic in family financial communications is the matter of sharing precise parental income with inquisitive offspring. Even parents willing to share all kinds of information with older children, to talk about the mortgage or financing a car or paying for college, still often hedge when it comes to disclosing the dollars and cents of income.

In families without much money, children may be vividly aware of the family's income and outgo. There is more of a matter-of-fact attitude toward money, fewer emotional connotations attached to money, sociologists claim, where survival is the issue. In more affluent families, however, parents sometimes bend over backwards to keep the children in ignorance of family finances. "It's hard for parents to be open and direct with children when our own sense of self-esteem, our place in the world, is tied in with monetary rewards," a family therapist points out. And, a parent observes, "asking how much money Daddy makes is like asking about your parents' sex life. It's just a taboo subject."

A lot of people, apparently, find money the same kind of conversational topic as sex—although some professional observers have commented that many adults are far more frank and candid about sex than about money. With children, though, both may be off limits. Ignorance does not breed competence, of course, in either area. In other homes, both sex and money may be talked about more openly and the children taught to manage both—which does not necessitate, in either case, revealing parental secrets. But some parents do consciously draw a parallel. "It's like sex," a Houston mother said when asked what they tell their children about the family income, "we don't sit down and talk about it, but when the children ask a question we tell them."

Yet most parents have good and ample reasons for not divulging their incomes. Young children, to begin with, despite their surface sophistication, simply cannot understand. One bright ten-year-old, daughter of an architect, kept pestering for an answer to "how much money do we have?" Finally, one evening, she said, "does Daddy make $7,000 a year?" After absorbing the amused looks around the dinner table, she asked, "Is that a lot?" Then, looking again, "Oh it's a little. Does he make a million dollars?" About all she discovered, finally, was that the answer was somewhere in between.

Most young children comprehend numbers with strings of zeroes as they comprehend arcane chemical formulae—not at all. Being able to read a number, like being able to recite the alphabet, has no bearing on comprehension. The child needs to understand money as a tool in his daily experience before he can understand large abstract sums. For a young child thousands of dollars are in the realm of the infinite and family income is a never-never land. Dr. Lisa Tallal states bluntly: "Young children can't visualize large sums. And it's really none of their business."

Furthermore, young children have a noticeable tendency to be indiscreet. "They would blab," one mother gently puts it. "In suburbia children talk too much. They come home and say 'so-and-so's mother is forty years old.' I don't want other children saying 'David's father earns such-and-such.' "

Most parents, agreeing, convey financial information in

broad general terms, sharing the costs that matter in a child's daily life, sharing a sense of priorities, but drawing the line at pinpointing income. "The children know, and we want them to know," says a Californian, "that we are better off than some, and less well off than others. That's all they have to know." As one father, addicted to spy stories, puts it: "I go by the whole cloak-and-dagger concept of 'need to know.' They have absolutely no need to know. When they're old enough to understand it's none of their business and when they're younger it doesn't matter."

Well-to-do parents who convince their children that they have little money, in an effort to avoid spoiled kids, can wind up with children fearful of spending. One thoroughly unhappy youngster, reported by a child psychologist, was literally terrified about having enough to eat—because her wealthy parents overemphasized the high cost of food and the necessity of eating every scrap. This is one extreme; the other, equally misconceived, is telling young children everything. They can't handle it. "I can't stand talking to Carol," says one ten-year-old. "She's always showing off. All she talks about is her swimming pool and her house and her clothes. Big deal. Who cares?"

The one exception to being purposely vague with small children was voiced by Benjamin Spock. "If something is worrying the family, the children need to know, on their own level. They will sense that something is going on—and with their vivid imaginations will worry much more about what they're not told than what they are." If expenses must be cut back for some reason—perhaps because a wage-earner is temporarily out of work—help the children to understand. But don't make them feel guilty over a situation they can't control; let them give up a movie if they really want to help, but don't let them stop eating lunch.

Sometimes children worry needlessly, misinterpreting adult conversation. Be sure you make things clear. "I remember falling asleep with a knot in the pit of my stomach," a woman now in her forties recalls. "I heard my father worrying about meeting mortgage payments, during the Depression, and thought we'd be put out on the street. Now, we've been complaining about food prices skyrocketing—and it suddenly occurred to me that my children might be getting worried. So I explained that, while we are concerned about the state of the economy, we are not in danger of going without food. We're cutting back on expensive steaks, sure, but we're not about to go hungry."

As children grow, as their horizons broaden, as they absorb their family's sense of values and priorities and as they become familiar with managing money of their own, they begin to sense more of the family's financial situation—whether or not you tell them. "Kids tuned in to the flow of family life can peg finances quickly and accurately," a school psychologist asserts. "Those who are tuned in to their parents, as well as to the world, know how much father makes, and know closely. Those not involved with the affairs of the family won't understand even if you give them a whole financial statement." "I don't believe in telling my income; there's absolutely no need for them to know," one father says, "but I bet he has a pretty good idea." Turning to the fourteen-year-old sprawled over the newspaper, he asks, "How much do we make? as a household?" The son, not looking up, replies "Oh, twenty or twenty-five." "That's low," the father says to me, "but it's a realistic, reasonable guess."

A banking executive agrees that this kind of general estimate is sufficient. Otherwise "it can put too much of a burden on the children. They should have a general idea but, even in high school, it's too early to share the cash flow of parents' income. What would be gained by it? Does it have any real meaning? If all the kids live in an affluent suburb, it's meaningless. If it's a very mixed-income area, it's a problem."

On the other hand, adolescents can bitterly resent being kept in ignorance when there are family problems. If sheltering small children is a mistake, as Dr. Spock insists, shielding teen-agers can be catastrophic. "I've encountered a number of very angry adolescents," says Robert Steinmuller, assistant clinical professor of psychiatry at the Albert Einstein College of Medicine in New York. "Their affluent parents, under stress with financial difficulty, 'protect' the youngsters. The kids know there is trouble but feel left out. They are angry about their parents' fear of leveling with them, telling the unpalatable truth, as if the kids couldn't understand. Sometimes they act out their anger by overspending. If they're brought into the adult world, the situation explained to them, they can settle down and be cooperative."

And, too, some parents feel strongly that an understanding of family finances is simply good for children. "We've always been very open with our children," says one. "I remember Ned, at fourteen, looking over my shoulder as I was paying bills. He commented that it looked like a lot of money we had. 'So it is,' I said, 'but look at what comes out of it for taxes, mortgage, insurance. There's not much left over.' Ned understood. He never bugged us for money."

Some adolescents are anxious to know parental income; others, taking family circumstances for granted, are not the least bit curious. I asked three Paramus, New Jersey, high school seniors whether they knew their family's income and got three sharply different answers. "I don't think I really want to know," said one; "I understand there's a certain limit on what we can have and can't have." "It's not a big deal in my family," said another, "I know the financial situation." And, said the third: "I've always wanted to know what my father makes. He won't tell, and says he won't ever. He just says, 'Are you happy? What's the difference what I make?' I did have to mark a bracket on my college application—it was so broad that I could guess it that roughly—but I really would like to know."

Would telling him, parents wonder, do anything but satisfy idle curiosity? There are times when sharing financial information seems futile in terms of actual understanding. "My nineteen-year-old son has absolutely no concept of dollars and cents, even though I told him my income," a New York businessman complains. "It's my fault, because he's never had to work for anything—I didn't want him to have to work the way I did—and that's the only way you really understand." Another parent confirms the belief that understanding develops through experience: "Now that my son dropped out of college and is working, he's suddenly very interested in money. I asked him if he was planning to save up, to buy the car he's been bugging us for since he was twelve. 'Mom,' he says, 'cars are expensive; I don't really need one.' I talked for years to that kid about how expensive cars are, and I never made a dent. Now that he has to use his money, he's decided he doesn't need a car after all. Even better," she goes on, "he asked me if I'd heard the President's news conference. This was a kid who's never been interested in such things. But he explained his sudden interest: 'You know, I got my first paycheck and they took out forty dollars for taxes. I've got to find out what they're doing with all that money.'"

Perhaps real understanding only comes from earning and managing substantial sums. "It's real future shock for kids," says an advertiser whose message is aimed at young people, "to realize the relationship between work and money."

But it needn't be total future shock. With honest parent-child communication in all the growing-up years, with an understanding of setting priorities, making decisions based on the best purchase at the best price, living on and not beyond the money available, children can be prepared to live in the real world.

13:
Summing Up

Living in the real world involves the use of money. We can't get away from it. Neither can we, really, get away from our own idiosyncrasies, the attitudes toward money ingrained in us over a lifetime.

In raising our children, sometimes we exaggerate our own early conditioning, sometimes we react in the opposite extreme to the things our parents taught us. We may want to spend freely, because our parents did not, and find ourselves emotionally unable to do so; others, with similarly self-denying parents, may spend very freely indeed. We may expect our children to make their own way because we had to. Or we may deliberately indulge our children because we were not indulged. Sometimes we regret the results. "My daughter says, 'Oh, that didn't cost much, only forty or fifty dollars,'" says one mother who admits to overindulgence, "and I get all upset."

Often we are inconsistent. We punish the petty dishonesty of children—and tell the bus driver they're still half fare. We tell them to defer gratification, to save and stretch their weekly pittance—while we buy what we want when we want it. We counsel them on the evils of debt—and charge as we go. We tell them not to worry about what the next kid has—and talk, loud and clear, about the neighbor's new car.

But, despite our inconsistencies, despite our inability to spend and save, at all times, the way we would like to, we can teach our children to do things right, to manage money wisely and well. They can live with our peculiarities about money, in fact, as they live with our other irrationalities and inconsistencies, and come out all right—if we manage to demonstrate a balanced attitude, a commonsense view of money as a highly useful item, but one divorced as much as possible from emotional connotations. We may spend money foolishly, in other words, or hoard it, but we should try not to bribe our children, not to confuse money with love, not to get them tied up in emotional knots over the use of money.

Such knots are positively Gordian; long-lasting and virtually impossible to undo, they become tighter with time. "Attitudes toward money in the early years," says Sondra K. Gorney, executive director of the Information Center on the Mature Woman, "are exaggerated in the middle years." The child who holds on to his money, unable to bring himself to spend it, unable to decide on anything worth parting with his money for, may become the adult unable to enjoy good fortune. The youngster trained to conserve, to deny present enjoyment for future security, may, as a mature adult, go into an emotional tailspin at the prospect of enjoying retirement, of taking the trip around the world he saved and planned for throughout his working years. And the child who throws money around, recklessly unable to defer gratification, to build security, may wind up as an adult on a treadmill, running furiously to stay in place.

Far more important than giving children allowances, far more important than encouraging them to spend and save with care, is our basic attitude of moderation. This means, whatever our income level, avoiding compulsive saving and its counterpart, heedless spending. It means showing children, as well as saying to them, that the good things in life are to be enjoyed but not wasted. "We make a point of not wanting to heat all outdoors, not leaving all the lights on, turning off the TV when no one is watching," says one Ohio father. Many parents have long tried to teach this simple lesson, to teach children not to be profligate, but it's been a difficult task in a world awash in affluence. The energy crisis of 1974 may have turned the tide. "My teen-agers have stopped taking the car out for small errands, and lights no longer burn in our house in unoccupied rooms," an Illinois reader wrote to *Good Housekeeping*. "Before this crisis, I found it was futile to try to enforce moderation. How can you argue scarcity with children who grew up in an age that acted as if 'there's always more where this came from.' "

In my growing-up years, it was just plain wasteful to leave lights burning or throw anything away unfinished. The "now" generation, without the "benefits" of Depression-conditioned parents or world-war shortages has been led to believe, until today, by society if not by parents, that resources are limitless and that we can afford them in endless amounts. Now we, all of us, know better.

Linked with the energy crisis, and with runaway inflation, in breaking this pattern of constant consumption, is youngsters' fervent desire to protect and conserve the environment, their interest in all things natural, from handcrafts to organic foods. Even small children understand that paper comes from trees and being profligate with paper means fewer forests, that plastic wrappings are nonrecyclable and it is therefore preferable to avoid excessive packaging. These are beliefs, especially if reinforced by parents, that convey the importance of moderation in life in general and in financial affairs in particular.

And children can be taught to comprehend the relationship between money, time and goods, even if on a minimal level. "Johnny thought that seventy-five cents was nothing to spend on an ice cream soda when I paid for it. When it had to come out of his allowance, he thought twice." This is an argument for (1) making allowances large enough so that they can cover reasonable expenditures, so that children can learn this relationship (a child who gets a quarter can never buy his own ice cream soda, not without enormously overrating its importance) and (2) encouraging youngsters to earn, even nominal amounts. The kid who has raked leaves or washed cars to earn a couple of dollars, who buys an ice cream soda out of his own earnings, has a firmer grip on reality, on the things money can do, than the youngster whose dollars come solely and endlessly from his parents.

While parental income as such may be none of the kids' business, for many good and valid reasons, they can learn a lot from having some idea of family expenditures, on a level appropriate to their age and understanding—again, not mortgage amounts but, perhaps, the cost of their own clothing. One mother of six insists: "They *should* know how much camp and braces and nursery school cost."

Yes, they should know what things cost—but not if the information is conveyed in a spirit of "Look how much we do for you." They should know what things cost—but as an educational device, a way to help them comprehend value for money, to cope with the real world, not as a weapon in an incessant battle for love.

"Worst of all," says psychiatrist Lisa Tallal, "is the underhanded punitive message many parents transmit: we sacrificed for you. Parents sacrifice for their children because it gives them pleasure; children don't owe them anything in return. I have a real gripe with the parent who expects a 'thank you.' What they really want is a warm bond with their children; you don't get it by making somebody angry and guilty."

They should know what things cost—but not if conveyed in a spirit of "Look what I did without so that you may have." There are adults who find it easy to spend on their children but very difficult to buy anything for themselves; they cannot seem to justify their own needs. But this is not the child's problem, and making him feel guilty for it is a mistake. "It becomes very confusing," says a family counselor, "to have a parent deprive herself and give to you. It doesn't make for any real sense of comfort in the family."

Furthermore, in families where real necessities are not at stake—that's quite another story—self-deprivation is hypocrisy. Children sense this and it makes them ill at ease. "I would much rather my mother had gotten a new coat instead of endlessly talking about how she was doing without. I felt so guilty," a Texas woman says of her childhood.

Similar resentment can build up when a mother does buy for herself—yet suspects, deep down, that she shouldn't. "After telling Christine that she couldn't have a new party dress, which she didn't need at all, I felt terrible about buying myself a suit I wanted." What is really happening here is that money, once again, has become a symbol for love. The new party dress denied the child seems, to the mother, to be love denied the child—which, of course, is nonsense. Unless parents measure love in this manner, children never learn to do so.

Why shouldn't parents buy things for themselves? The self-sacrificing parent in a child-centered family does no favors to anyone, child or adult. Like the Texas woman whose mother denied herself a coat "for the sake of the children," the end result is resentment. Far better a commonsense approach, like the mother who says, "I don't have to justify my spending to the children, or make apologies for denying them anything. If I think a request for guitar lessons, or new and unnecessary clothes, is a frivolous fancy—or simply one that the budget won't absorb at the moment—I just say so. But that has absolutely nothing to do with what I spend or don't spend on myself."

What it comes down to, in the end, is family values. If we, ourselves, set priorities, buying what is important at a given time within what the budget can tolerate, our children will learn to do so. They can learn, too, that their needs and wants do not inevitably come first, that the family as a unit and the parents as individuals have needs and wants which frequently take precedence—and that the family is a unit which works together.

What children, and adults, need above all is honesty. It doesn't hurt children to know that adult interests often come first. It doesn't hurt children to see that we are human, with human inconsistencies; they see our feet of clay soon enough, and accuse us of hypocrisy. Far better to be honest and open about our failings. And it doesn't hurt children when we admit that money is important. The old wives' tale that money does not buy happiness is, today, nothing short of ridiculous. Even the simplest pleasures are impossible without money. I vividly recall the time a day of hiking and climbing in a state park cost us over twenty dollars, for tolls and gasoline and the makings of a picnic lunch. It's difficult to go anywhere, or do anything, without some money. So let's be honest, with our children and with ourselves, about money's place in our lives.

Money *is* important. Without it, it is hard to be happy. We do not want to overemphasize its importance, to the point where we, and our children, become overmaterialistic, to the point where we confuse money with love and approval and security. But ignoring its importance, playing it down, is equally unrealistic and unhealthy. Money is a necessary commodity in our culture, essential for the provision of food and clothing and shelter and the pleasures that make life worth living. That's the point: money itself has absolutely no value. Its value lies solely in the things it can provide, as a medium of exchange.

The only way any of us ever learned to manage money, to handle large sums and comprehend their buying power, really, is to do so: to pay rent, buy food, finance a car, invest. The same will be true for our children. Their knowledge of finance on any but the most basic level will, and must, remain abstract until they leave the nest and fly. But we can pave the way, help them flutter their wings in preliminary encounters with the world, by giving them some money to manage, encouraging them to earn more, and above all else, encouraging them, through our own attitudes and actions, to regard money, that symbol of symbols, as nothing more—and nothing less—than a useful, highly useful, tool.

Selected Readings

* Acknowledgment is gratefully given for the use of material from these books.

CHILD DEVELOPMENT

Beadle, Muriel. *A Child's Mind*. Doubleday. Garden City, New York, 1970

*Bossard, James H. and Eleanor Stoker Boll. *The Sociology of Child Development*. Harper & Row, New York, 1960.

Erikson, Erik H. *Childhood and Society*. W.W.Norton & Co., New York, 1950, 1963.

Fraiberg, Selma. *The Magic Years*. Charles Scribner's Sons, New York, 1959.

Gesell, Arnold, M.D. and Frances L. Ilg, M.D. *Child Development: The Child From Five to Ten*. Harper & Row, New York. 1949.

Gruenberg, Sidonie. *Parent's Guide to Everyday Problems of Boys and Girls*. Random House, New York, 1958.

Ilg, Frances L., M.D. and Louise Bates Ames. *Child Behavior*. Dell Publishing Co., New York, 1955, 1960.

LeShan, Eda. *How to Survive Parenthood.* Random House, New York, 1965.

*Salk, Lee, M.D. *What Every Child Would Like His Parents To Know.* David McKay, New York, 1972.

ADOLESCENCE

Coleman, James. *The Adolescent Society.* The Free Press of Glencoe, New York. 1961.

*Josselyn, Irene M., M.D. *Adolescence.* Harper & Row, New York, 1971.

*Keniston, Kenneth. *The Uncommitted.* Harcourt Brace Jovanovich, New York, 1965.

*Keniston, Kenneth. *Youth and Dissent.* Harcourt Brace Jovanovich. New York, 1960, 1971.

*Klein, Alexander, editor. *Natural Enemies???* J.B. Lippincott, Philadelphia, 1969.

Mead, Margaret. *Culture and Commitment. A Study of the Generation Gap.* Natural History Press/Doubleday. Garden City, New York, 1970.

Sebald, Hans. *Adolescence. A Sociological Analysis.* Appleton-Century-Croft. New York, 1968.

DIFFERENCES OF GENDER

Bardwick, Judith. *Psychology of Women.* Harper & Row, New York, 1971.

Bird, Caroline. *Born Female.* David McKay, New York, 1968.

*Maccoby, Eleanor E., editor. *The Development of Sex Differences.* Stanford University Press, Stanford, California. 1966.

Mead, Margaret. *Male and Female.* William Morrow, New York, 1949.

THE PSYCHOLOGY OF MONEY

*Bergler, Edmund, M.D. *Money and Emotional Conflicts.* International Universities Press, Inc., New York. 1959, 1970.

Brown, Norman O. *Life Against Death.* Vintage Books, New York. 1959.

Lauterbach, Albert. *Man, Motives and Money.* Cornell University Press, Ithaca, New York. 1959.

*Knight, James A., M.D. *For the Love of Money.* J.B.Lippincott, Philadelphia, Pa. 1968.

SOCIOLOGY

*Bettelheim, Bruno. *Children of the Dream.* Macmillan, New York. 1969

Bird, Caroline. *The Invisible Scar.* David McKay, New York. 1966.

Cameron, Mary Owen. *The Booster and the Snitch.* Macmillan, New York, 1964.

Feldman, Frances Lomas. *The Family in a Money World.* Family Service Association of America, New York. 1957.

*Ginzburg, Eli, editor. *The Nation's Children* (three volumes) Columbia University Press, New York. 1960.

Gordon, Richard E., Katherine K. Gordon and Max Gunther. *The Split-Level Trap.* Random House, New York. 1961.

Klemer, Richard H. *Marriage and Family Relationships.* Harper & Row, New York. 1970.

Kohn, Melvin. *Class and Conformity: A Study in Values.* Dorsey, Homewood, Illinois. 1969.

Lear, Martha Weinman. *The Child Worshippers.* Crown Publishers, New York. 1963.

Mead, Margaret. *And Keep Your Powder Dry.* William Morrow, New York, 1942.

Packard, Vance. *The Status Seekers.* David McKay, New York. 1959.

*Riesman, David. *The Lonely Crowd.* Yale University Press. New Haven, 1950, 1953.

Toffler, Alvin. *Future Shock.* Bantam Books, New York. 1970.

ADVERTISING AND MARKETING

Black, Hillel. *Buy Now, Pay Later.* William Morrow, New York. 1961.

Britt, Steuart Henderson. *Consumer Behavior in Theory and in Action.* John Wiley & Sons, Inc. New York. 1970.

*Gilbert, Eugene. *Advertising and Marketing to Young People.* Printers' Ink Books. Pleasantville, New York. 1957.

Liebert, Robert M., John M. Neale & Emily S. Davidson. *The Early Window.* Pergamon. 1973.

*Sheldon, Eleanor Bernert, editor. *Family Economic Behavior.* J.B. Lippincott, Philadelphia. 1973.

Index

About the Author

Grace Weinstein's articles—on child development, money management, education, family relationships, mental health—have appeared in many national publications, among them *Money Magazine, Saturday Review/World, House Beautiful, Parents' Magazine, Family Weekly, Scholastic Teacher.*

Ms. Weinstein is a graduate of Cornell University. She lives in Teaneck, New Jersey with her husband, an architect, and their two children.

#2284-17
1976
5-04
C